Do It With iPad - A Practical iPad Manual For Complete iPad Guide

Contents

Introduction

About The Author

My name is Mike, and for nearly 9 years, I enjoyed a successful career working in a apple store in the city of London as part of the Theatre & Events team.My job was to deliver hardware and software workshops, demonstrating how to use Apple products. This would be to a live audience of people of all ages and levels of experience. This would often involve 1 hour 'Getting Started with iPad' and 1 hour 'Going Further with iPad' sessions, covering essential areas of iOS, iCloud, iPad settings etc.

Getting Started With iPad

Setting up the iPad

When you first get an iPad, you will need to do a few things to get it up and running. Press the power button to switch on and then slide your finger from left to right on the screen to unlock the iPad. You will be asked to input your preferred language, country and origin.

Next, you will be presented with an option to disable or enable Location Services. This can be changed later on, but if you would like to use your iPad to locate yourself on a map, track it if you happen to lose it, or add locations to your photos, I would recommend adding it now. You'll find it in your "Settings" if you wish to change it later.

Click next, and then select a WiFi network you would like to connect to. A WiFi network is required to activate your iPad, unless you plug it into iTunes. If your network requires a password, you will be asked to enter it after clicking on the network name. You'll also be able to alter your WiFi settings on the "Settings" page.

On the next screen, you will be asked if you want to set up the iPad as a brand new one, or restore it from an iCloud or iTunes backup. If you have ever downloaded songs through iTunes, or used iCloud on another iOS or Mac device, you will already have an Apple ID and you can sign in here. If you don't, click on Create a Free Apple ID and follow the registration process.

Once you have signed in, click 'agree' to accept the Terms and Conditions, and then your iPad will connect to Apple's server to be activated. Once your iPad is activated, you will be asked if you want to use iCloud. iCloud is a free service which gives you a free email account, allows you to track your iPad if you lost it, and syncs most of your content between your iOS and Mac devices. You might already have an iCloud account. You will be able to access this on your new iPad by inputting your iCloud ID and password. If you choose not to to do this now, you can set up your iCloud account at any time by pressing the settings icon on the home screen

If you do choose to use iCloud, you can now decide if you want to back it up to iCloud or iTunes. If you select the iCloud, your iPad will automatically back itself up every night when it's connected to power, so you won't have to worry about it. If not, you will be required to sync to iTunes if you wish to back up your content.

You will be asked if you want to use iCloud's "Find My iPad". This is a free service, which allows you to track and send messages to your iPad if you lose it. You'll be asked if you want to enable Siri which is Apple's voice command system. It allows you to speak rather than type your commands

You'll also be asked if you want to use the iCloud's keychain, which allows you to import passwords from other devices and if you do, you'll be prompted to enter a passcode. Finally, you can decide whether or not to send Diagnostics to Apple. Diagnostics are completely anonymous, and allow Apple to improve their products, but this is entirely up to you. Just click on "Start Using iPad", and it is now ready for you to use!

Different buttons

Overview

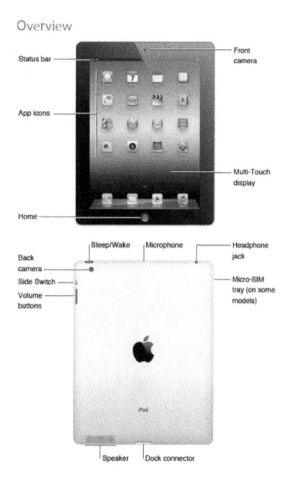

On the front of the iPad, you will see a small FaceTime camera lens, This camera is used for making video calls. You'll also see the home button. Regardless of what you're looking at, the home button will return you to the home screen. This button can also be used to activate Siri and open the multitasking bar. When pressed three times spoken support for the visually impaired will be activated and if held down, the set up assistant will be activated, should you need to reboot your iPad.

On the top of the iPad there is a lock button, a microphone, and a headphone jack. The lock button is used to either, as the name suggests, lock the iPad so the display is no longer active, or, if you press and hold it, turn the iPad off. On the right hand side, there is a mute switch and a volume rocker. You can prevent the iPad from making sounds by activating the mute switch, and turn the volume up and down using the rocker. If you want to quickly turn the volume right down, you can press and hold the volume down button.

On the bottom of the iPad, is the dock connector. On the latest iPad and iPad Mini, this will be a smaller, Thunderbolt connector, but on the other iPads, it will be the 30-pin connector shown shown here. This is used to charge the iPad up, to connect it to iTunes, and to play music on docking systems. Finally, on the back of the iPad, you will find an iSight camera you can use to take photos with your iPad.

Arranging icons and home screen

New apps that are downloaded will be accessible via the corresponding icons which will appear on the home screen. When they first appear, you won't have any say over the position of the icons. However, it's easy enough to rearrange them. Select the icon you want to move and when all the icons start jiggling about, drag your selected icon to its new home screen location. If you want to move an icon to a different page, hold and slide the icon either to the extreme left or right of the screen, depending on which page you want to move it to. The icon can then be repositioned on its new page.

Icons can be dragged into and out of the dock as well. The dock is the shortcut menu bar which appears at the bottom of the screen. The dock is used for apps which you use often. The iPad has room for 6 dock icons. When you have finished rearranging the home screen, press the home button.

When you download a lot of apps, you might find that your home screen starts to look cluttered. You can group similar apps together in folders in order to make your home screen appear neater, as well as reduce the number of icons on it. To create a folder, you simply need to drag one icon on top of another. A folder will be created and named automatically. This folder will contain the two icons. Drag as many additional icons as you want into the folder. The folder can then be renamed by selecting it and holding it until it jiggles. When it does this, tap it, and then you will be able to change the folder's name. Apps can be dragged out of the folder, in the same way they were dragged in, by selecting them and dragging.

Finger Gestures

Tap

Briefly touch surface with fingertip

Double tap

Rapidly touch surface twice with fingertip

Drag

Move fingertip over surface without losing contact

Flick

Quickly brush surface with fingertip

Pinch

Touch surface with two fingers and bring them closer together

Spread

Touch surface with two fingers and move them apart

Press

Touch surface for extended period of time

Press and tap

Press surface with one finger and briefly touch surface with second finger

Press and drag

Press surface with one finger and move second finger over surface without losing contact

Rotate

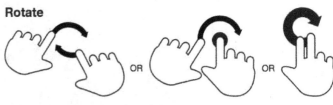

Touch surface with two fingers and move them in a clockwise or counterclockwise direction

One of the most important skills you really need to use your iPad, is to understand finger gestures. As you know, there are no buttons on the front of the device, other than the Home button. So the majority of the things you'll do, are accomplished by tapping, sliding, rotating, or pinching your fingers on the screen. There are only a few basic moves, but they're part of the DNA of using iPad, and it's essential to really learn them well. The most basic gesture is the tap and it's just what it sounds like. You tap a part of your screen to perform some action. For example, You can tap on any of the applications to run them.

Let's take "Photos" as an example. You're in your photo library and you select the album you want to look at, again, by tapping. You'll find yourself looking at thumbnails of all the photos in this album. The next gesture is the drag. Again this is just what it sounds like.To browse through these photos, you keep your finger in contact with the screen and drag the thumbnails up and down. If you run out of room as you're dragging your finger, you can just lift it up and place it back at the top of the screen to continue dragging.

Closely associated with the drag gesture is the flick. Imagine you're on a long page on the Safari web browser. Dragging over and over again can get really tedius, especially if you have a lot of content to scroll through. So instead, lift your finger off the screen as you reach the end of the drag.

You'll notice that the content on the screen continues to move. The nice thing about flicking is that it's speed sensitive. So you can flick slowly, to browse at a leisurely pace or, if you know the content you want to look at is somewhere near the bottom, you can flick quickly to get there faster.

The next gesture is the pinch. Think about the photos again. This is when you touch two fingers, usually your thumb and index fingers, to the screen. Then either separate them, which as you can see zooms in on the picture, or bring them back together, which zooms back out. This is referred to as pinching in and pinching out. It doesn't matter which two fingers you use. Now, while zoomed in on a photo, you can use the drag gesture as well as the flick gesture. If you're not zoomed in, dragging and flicking will take you from photo to photo. The tap, the drag, the flick, and pinching in an out, are really the most basic and commonly used gestures on iOS devices.

Now there are additional variations on these moves. For example, a quick double-tap on an item often zooms in on it. In photos, it zooms in on the picture. If you're browsing a website in Safari, double tapping a column of text zooms that column to the width of your screen. There's also multi-finger tapping, which appears in apps like "Maps". Double tapping zooms in like you'd expect. But to zoom out, you can just single tap with two fingers. Pinching in and out is available here as well. Some apps require you not to tap but to touch and hold an on-screen button to make it work.

When you touch and hold any of the icons on your home screen it puts them into organization mode. You can then drag the icons from location to location to re-arrange them as you want. Pressing the Home button will turn that off. Another trick is scrolling. If you scroll down through a lot of context and you want to get back to the top of the screen, rather than having to flick the screen multiple times, you can simply tap the top of the screen. You'll be instantly scrolled back up. This doesn't work in every single app but many of them do work this way. And you might come across other options that iPad app developers have programmed into their apps like two finger dragging, two finger rotating, and so on.

Generally, you'll be taught which gestures to use by the instructions that come with the app. There you have the basic finger gestures you need to know to really use the iPad efficiently.

Multitasking and Multitasking Gestures

Multitasking is an feature that allows apps to perform certain tasks in the background while you are using another app. It allows you to switch instantly between apps and to resume an app. If you are currently in an app and wish to switch to another, you can either return to the home screen and tap on it, or you can double press the home button to display recently used apps. This causes the screen to display a row of app cards which are currently open and running in the background. You can tap on any of these app cards to switch to that app quickly and can pick up where you left off.

The way you close an app by sliding its app card. Another little trick you can do is to actually clear up two or three Apps at a time just by swiping up using two fingers or three fingers.

In addition to using the home button to activate the multitasking card display, you can use multitasking gestures. To return to the home screen, pinch with four or five fingers, and the app will close. Swiping upwards with four fingers will cause the screen to shift and multitasking card display will appear. Swiping left or right with four fingers when in an app will allow you to quickly switch between your recently-used apps.

These hand gestures can make using the iPad a little bit quicker and easier, but if you don't want to use them or find them interfering with your apps, you can turn them off by opening the "Settings" app, navigating to the "General" section and turning the "Multitasking Gestures" switch off.

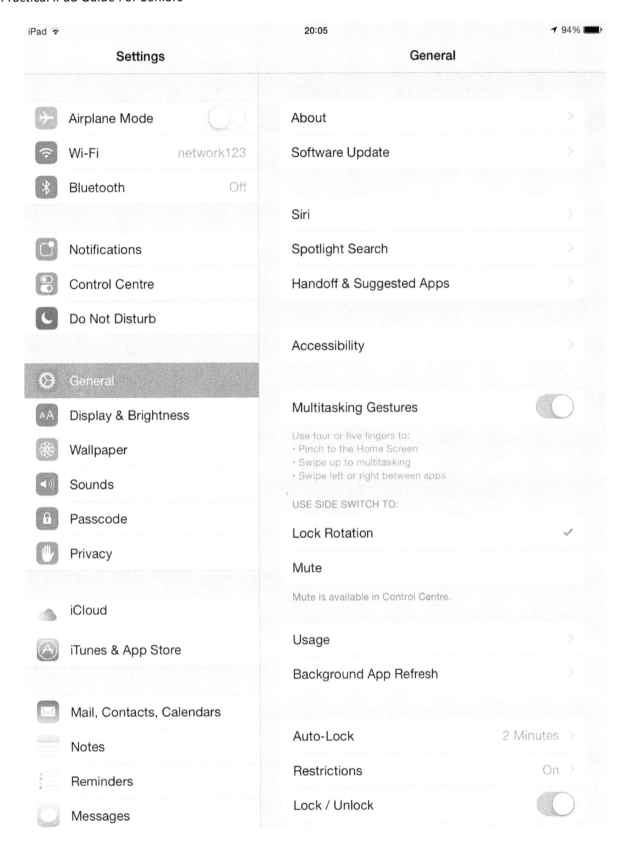

This will only switch off the multitasking gestures. You can still access the multitasking cards by double pressing the home button.

Controlling Sounds

One of the first things you'll want to get under control on your iPad is the default sounds and their volume levels. Given that you can set and turn on specific sounds for specific events and actions, you'll want to select, or at least familiarize yourself with these sounds, so you'll know what your device is trying to tell you. Locate and tap the "Settings" icon to open your iPad system settings. And then locate and tap "Sounds".

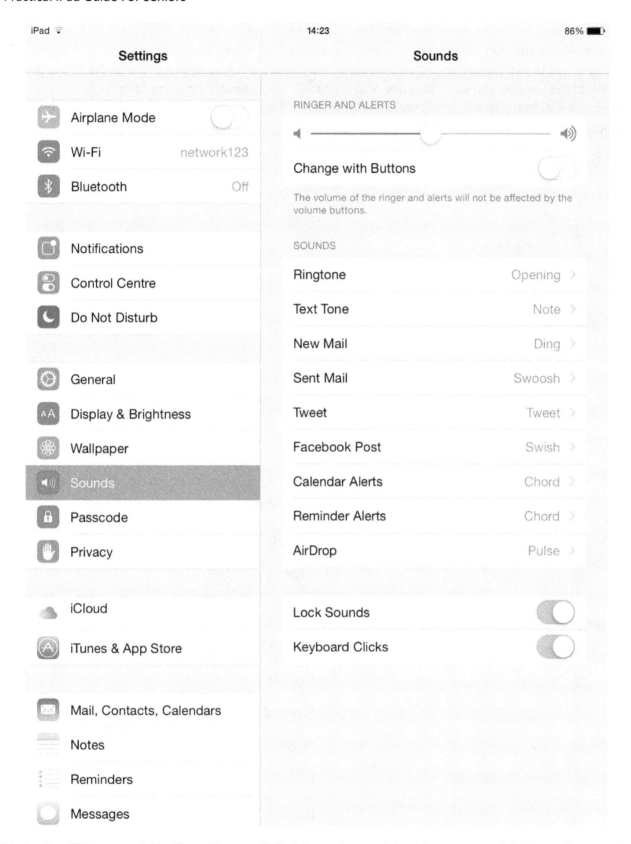

Under the "Ringer and Alert" section, you'll find the volume slider. You can use this to set the overall volume of your ringtones and other sounds. Either drag the slider on screen or use the volume controls on the side of the iPad and you'll see the slider move itself. Now if the slider doesn't move when you press the buttons, make sure the "Change with Buttons" switch is turned on. However, some people prefer to keep this off, so that the volume buttons only control other sounds like the volume level of games or movies.

Another setting is the ringtone selector. This is where you can determine the sound that plays when someone calls you. On this screen, you'll find all of the iPad's built in sounds under the "Ringtones" setting. Any custom ringtones you've created or purchased will also appear here at the top of this list. All of the sounds you see listed are new on iOS 7. If you have a ringtone from a previous version of iOS that you like, you'll find it under Classic. Tap on any of the sounds to sample and select them.

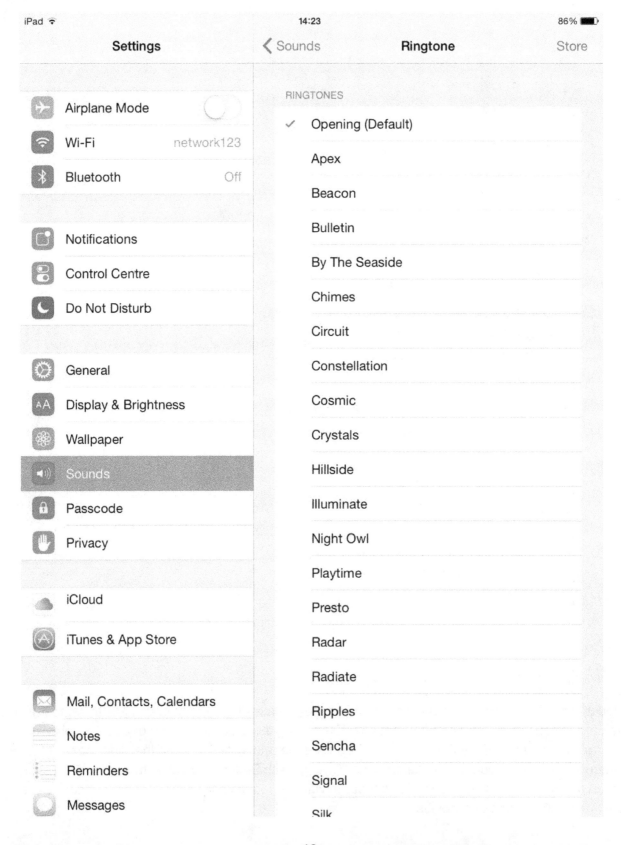

And you'll also find a section called Alert Tones, which are generally short sounds that are used for things like text messages, incoming mail, and other alerts. These are also all new to iOS 7. And you'll find another classic folder containing all the older alert sounds.

Set the alert sounds as you would set a ringtone. You get the same selection of sounds here as you did under ringtones but the alert tones section is listed first. The rest of these options deal with what sounds play when certain events occur. You have New Voicemail, New Mail, Sent Mail, Tweet, Facebook Post, Calendar Alerts, Reminder Alerts and AirDrop. Just select and browse through the same sounds as before. Note that you can also choose "None" if you prefer your device to make no sound at all when one of these events occurs.

The lock sound is what you hear when you press the Sleep Wake button And keyboard clicks are the typing sound you hear when you're using your devices' keyboard. You can turn these two options on and off, but you can't change their sounds.

These are the sound settings. Take some time to listen to each sound, so you know what they represent. And as you get used to your iPad, you can come back in here and decide whether or not you want to hear any of these sounds.

Setting Rotation Lock / Mute Switch

You probably noticed that when you move your iPad around, its display rotates so that the object in front of you is always facing the right way up. You may also notice that the iPad will make noises when you don't want it to. There is a toggle switch on the side that can affect either of these behaviors, because it can be configured as a rotation lock. This means that regardless of how you move your iPad, the screen's display won't switch from one orientation to another. It can also be configured so that when you switch it on, the iPad's volume is immediately muted.

To choose the switches function, launch settings by tapping "Settings", look in the "General" setting, and finally find the "Use Side Switch" option.

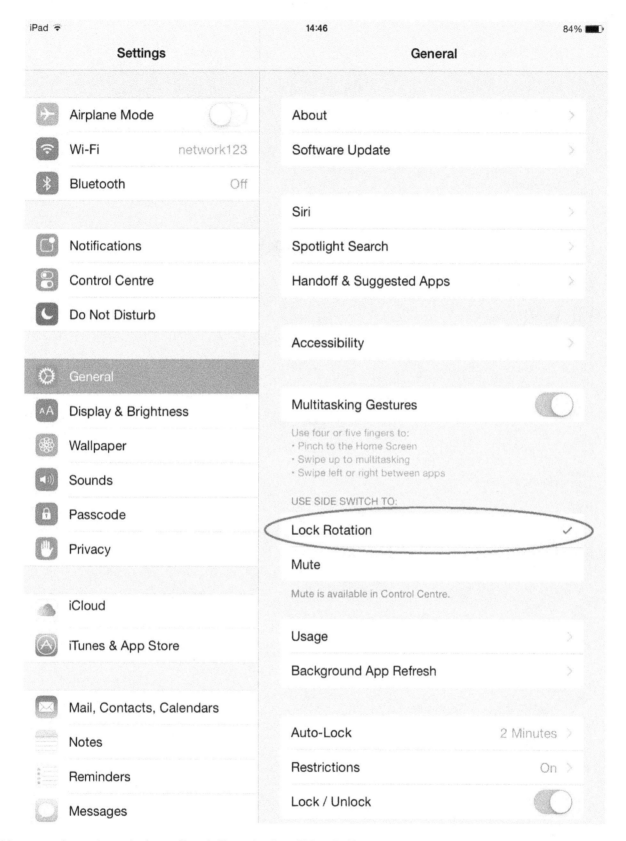

Here you have two choices: "Lock Rotation" or "Mute". If you set it to "Lock Rotation", you can rotate it and sure enough, it rotates.

When you then bring it back to landscape orientation and flip the switch, you can see the "Lock" icon.

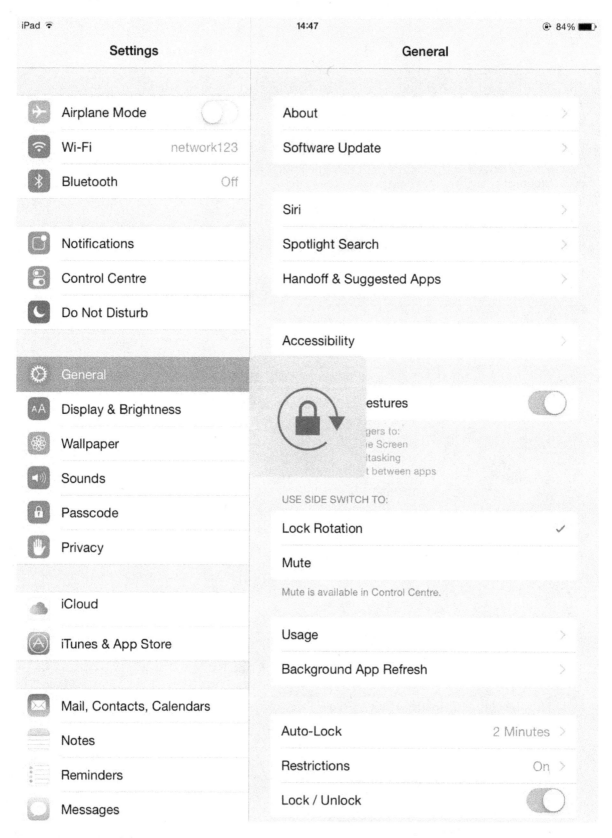

Rotate again and it doesn't move, so it really does work. Now flip it back, and you'll see that it can be rotated.

Autolock

The Auto-Lock feature refers to the iPad's default behaviour of turning off the screen after a minute or so of inactivity. It's useful because it guards you against accidentally tapping an icon or dialling a number from the iPhone while it's in your pocket. It's a great way to protect your iOS device from being accidentally used, or from being accessed by people you haven't authorized. It also acts as a good battery conservation feature. Having it in place will increase the chances of you getting your device back if you ever misplace it, or if it's stolen.

Here's how to use it. Go to "Settings" and then "General". Here you'll find Auto-Lock. You can choose to set it for 2 to 15 minutes, making it so that you have to press the Sleep/Wake button, and slide the unlock slider to use your device again. EG If your Autolock is set for 2 minutes, then after 2 minutes, you'll need to input your code again:

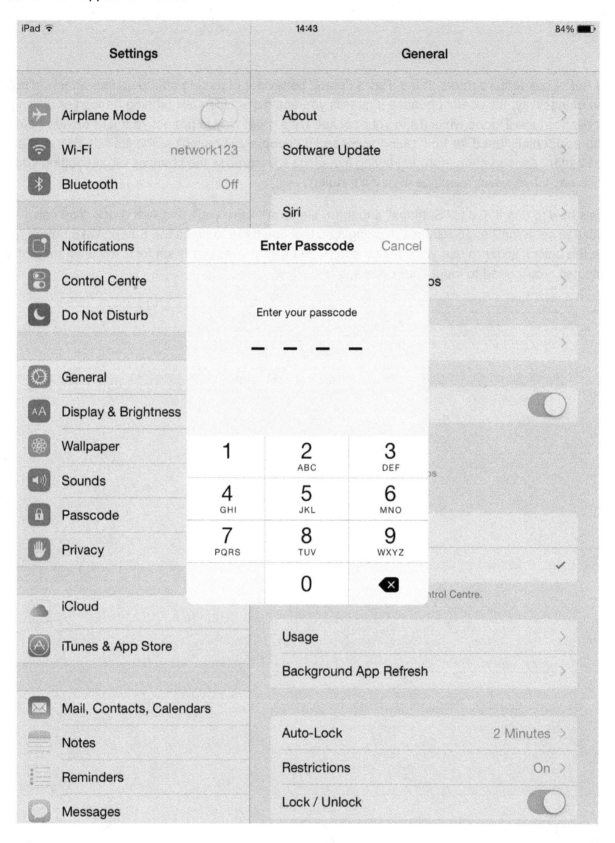

The choices are a two, five, ten, or 15 minute interval of inactivity before it locks the screen and here's where to change your Autolock options.

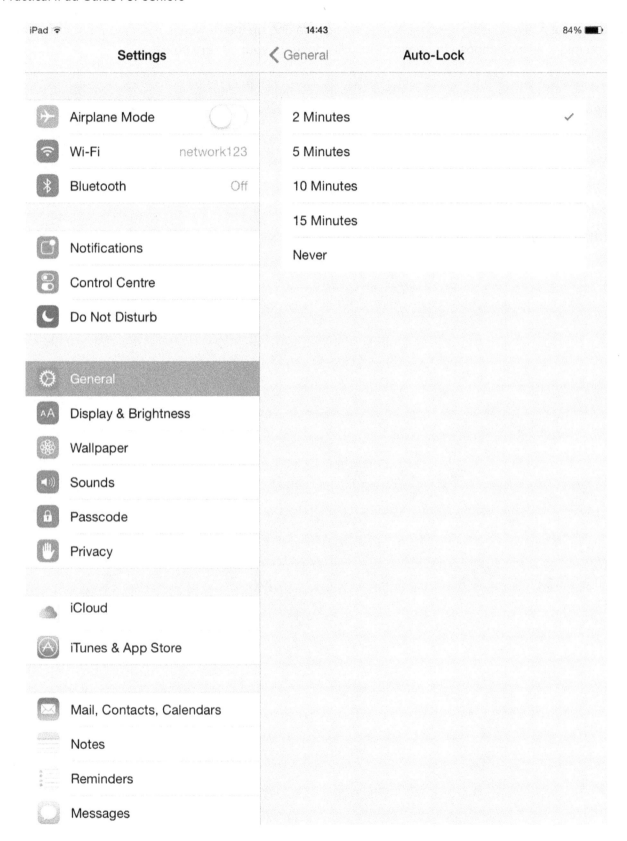

You can also choose "Never". This means the screen will stay on indefinitely until you lock it yourself with the Sleep/Wake button, or until it runs out of battery power.

Just remember that you have to manually lock your screen if you choose "Never". If you forget, your battery will drain much more quickly. I think the default setting of one minute, or maybe even two minutes are good settings to use. If you haven't touched your device in a one or two minutes, you're probably not actively using it, so let it go to sleep. Waking up the device is a simple matter anyway, so you might as well choose the option that will conserve your battery power.

Using Passcode Lock

If you keep personal information on your iPad, or if you just want to make sure that no one will be able to use your device by picking it up when it has been lost or stolen, it's a good idea to use the passcode feature found in "Settings".

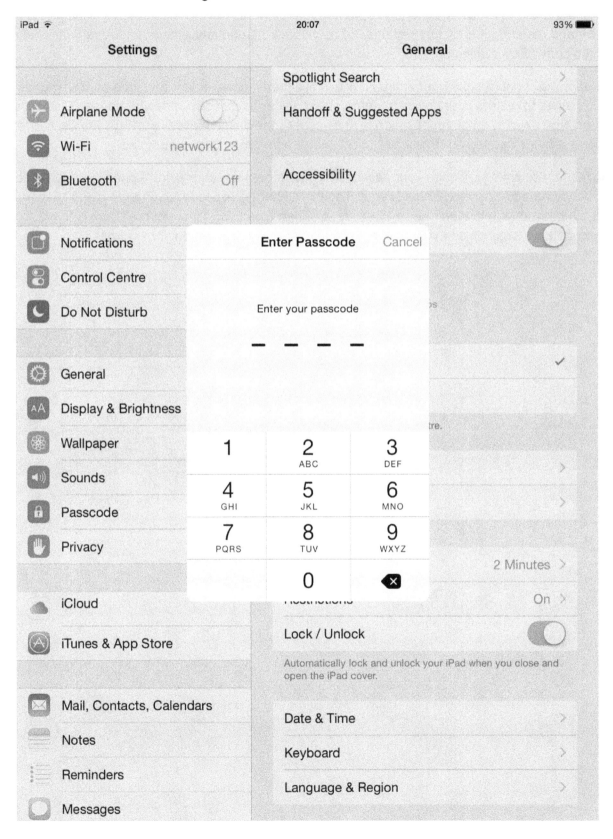

When using it for the first time, tap "Passcode On" and you'll be prompted to enter a four digit passcode. This is a four digit passcode of your choosing. Just tap one in, and then tap it again to confirm that you typed it correctly. Now at this point it's important to stress that you have turned "Passcode" on. Ie if you were to lock your screen right now, and then wake it up again, you'd be prompted to enter your passcode before you can access your phone. What I'm saying is, it's very, very, very important that you don't forget what this code is. If you forget your passcode, the only way to access the device again is to restore it in iTunes, which involves completely wiping the device and restoring it to factory settings. Of course, if you regularly sync your device, you'll have a backup copy of everything on it.

However, having to restore your entire device is still pretty inconvenient and time-consuming, so avoid having to restore your device by remembering your passcode. Once you have the passcode lock on, you need to enter your passcode to re-access the passcode lock settings. Go back to your general settings and tap on "Passcode Lock". You'll be prompted for that code.

You might also want to change your passcode if you're not sure your current passcode is secure. Maybe your friend or coworker guessed it. Tap on "Change Passcode" to change it. Firstly, type in your old passcode, and then enter a new one. Confirm it and you'll find yourself back into the Passcode Lock settings and your new passcode is now in effect. Again, don't forget it.

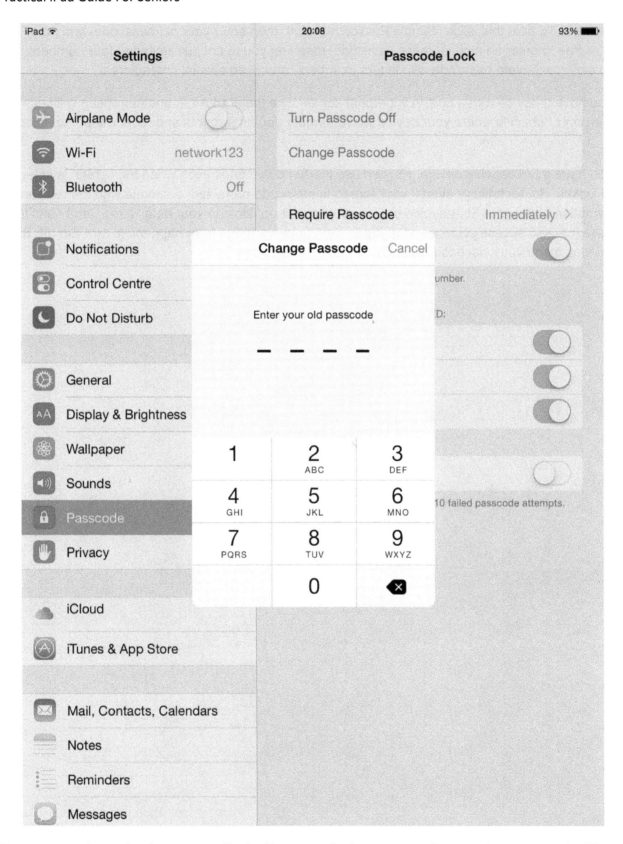

Next we can determine how soon after locking your device you want it to require a passcode. The default is immediately. As soon as you lock your screen, you'll have to enter your passcode again right away to wake it up. You can change this time limit to 1, 5, or 15 minutes, or even 1 or 4 hours. Obviously, shorter times are more secure.

A Simple passcode is the default four digit number system that we've been using so far, but if you're really serious about keeping your device secure, you might want to consider a more secure password. To alter this, slide "Simple Passcode" to off, then enter your old passcode, and now you're free to enter an alphanumeric passcode, meaning you're not just limited to four numbers. You can now have a passcode with letters, numbers, and even special characters.

If you have a device with a built-in fingerprint sensor, like the iPad Air 2, another option will be fingerprints, which is where your device will remember you fingerprints and require them to unlock it.

If you have a Siri capable device, you can use the Siri commands even when the screen is asleep and locked. So, technically even if your screen is passcode protected, someone with the relevant information about your Siri-enabled device could pick it up, look up your details, read and send text messages, and access your calendar. If you want to prevent that from happening, turn Siri off. But that does mean you'll have to unlock your iPad in order to use Siri.

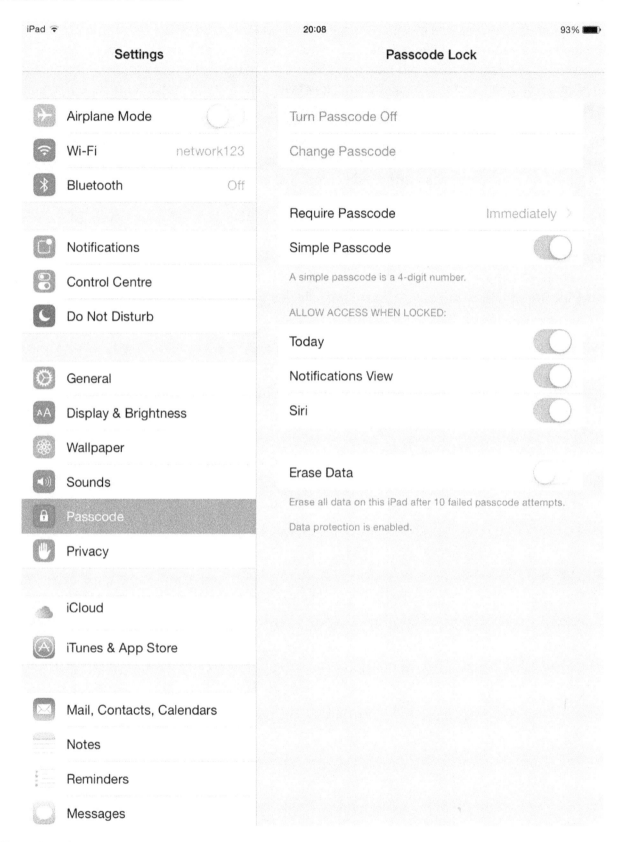

There is a final, serious option. If your iPad is stolen and you have it passcode protected, with "Erase Data" turned on, your device will automatically erase itself if someone unsuccessfully tries to unlock your phone ten times.

Some people have asked, "what if my kid picks up my phone and starts playing with it? If he starts typing numbers on the passcode he could erase my iPad?" However, there are actually significant safeguards built-in to prevent this sort of thing. After six unsuccessful attempts at entering the passcode you have to wait one minute before the iPad, will let you try again. After that, the waiting period increases each time to five minutes, 15 minutes, one hour, and then four hours. So you have to be deliberately trying to break into the device before you hit ten attempts and the iPad is erased. There's very little chance of that happening accidentally. Bear in mind that if the feature still makes you nervous, you can always leave "Erase Data" off.

Lastly, if you don't think you need the passcode protection and want to turn if off, just scroll back up to the top of "Settings" and tap, "Turn Passcode Off". You will get a warning screen, telling you that with it turned off, your safe passwords, credit cards, and important data can be viewed and used by anyone who has access to your iPad. If you want to take that chance, just tap "turn off." You'll have to enter your passcode one more time. If you've enabled "Safari AutoFill", which includes the ability to remember your website passwords and credit card information, if you've added it, you get the option to turn that off as well. I'd just choose keep using Safari AutoFill for now, but again if you're worried about security after turning off the passcode, you might want to consider turning that off and deleting the passwords. Once you've done that, your iPad, will be un-passcode protected.

Using Find My iPad

Let's face it, iPad is not cheap and if you keep a lot of sensitive information and important appointments on your device, misplacing or losing your iPad can be devastating. Fortunately, Apple offers a free service through iCloud called "Find My iPad". "Find My iPad" is a great security measure to have in place. Since it's free, there's really no reason to not set it up, because it offers you the ability to locate your missing or stolen device on a map. It also performs remote functions like passcode locking it or even completely erasing it all from a regular web browser. So how does it work?

Firstly, you'll need to make sure the device is set up to use "Find My iPad". Start by tapping on "Settings".

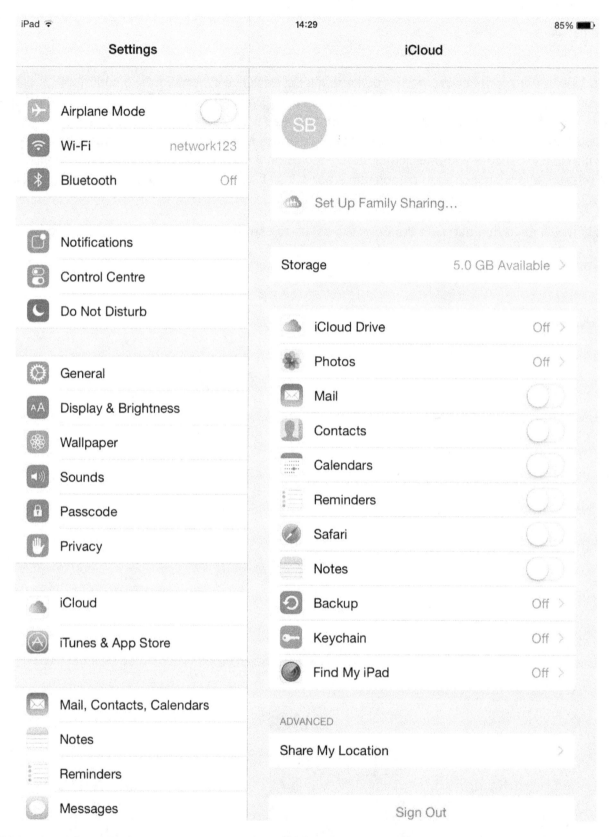

Then go to "iCloud". If you are subscriber to iCloud and have already previously set up your account, you'll find the "Find My iPad" switch near the bottom of the screen. You were probably even prompted to turn it on the first time you set up your iPad. If "Find My iPad" is not on, switch it on.

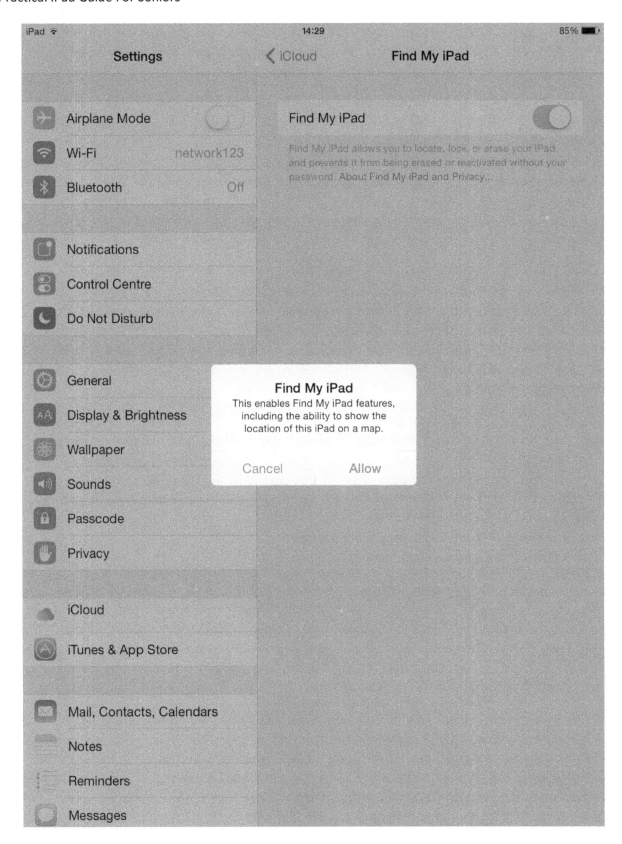

And once it's on, that's pretty much it. You can forget about it until the day you lose or misplace your phone. So if it ever happens that you lose your device or even misplace it somewhere in your home or office, go to icloud.com in your web browser and login with your Apple ID.

Then click the "Find My iPad" icon. After a moment, a map appears giving you the approximate location of your iPad or other device. If you have multiple devices, they'll all be listed under "All Devices", just select the one you want to locate. Now, if you have an iPad, or (if you lost it) had an iPad, the location should be just as accurate as when you get your location in the map program on the iPad. Wi-Fi only iPads will be slightly less accurate, but you should still be able to get the general idea of where your device is located within a radius of a few blocks, especially if it's in a location with lots of Wi-Fi signals.

Using the map, you might even be able to tell if your device is misplaced at home with you, or somewhere else. You can click the browser or "Refresh" button to have iCloud search for your phone again, which might be useful if someone stole your iPad and they're driving around with it. With this information, you could potentially let the police know the approximate location of your iPad. There have been several reports of Find My iPad, leading the police right to the person who stole the device. You will be shown a display, in the upper right hand corner of which, will tell you how long ago your device was located and show you its current battery level.

Below the image of the device are three buttons. The first one is "Play Sound". This lets you send a command to your iPad that makes it play a loud pinging sound, and the great thing about this is it works even if you left your iPad in silent mode. You can use this feature just to find where you left the iPad in my house. Just click "Play Sound" to immediately make your iPad start pinging. As long as your iPad is still on, it should start emitting a sound within seconds, and in cases where you know the iPad is in your house, you can start wandering around looking for it. You'll also received an email telling you that the sound was played on your iPad.

This will confirm that the sound did get through to the iPad, which might be useful if the iPad is actually lost and you can't find it, at least you'll know that it did make a sound some place and perhaps somebody will find it for you. The next button is "Lost Mode", this is used when you've actually lost your iPad and want to protect it from being used by someone else who just picks it up. Click "Lost Mode" and if your device isn't already passcode locked, you'll be prompted to enter a four digit pass code, to confirm it. This allows you to immediately lock your iPad. If your iPad is already protected by a pass code you'll see this screen first.

Here you can enter a number where anyone who finds your iPad can reach you. The default message reads this iPad has been lost please call me. Click "Done". In a few seconds a message appear will appear on your iPad. Anybody who finds my iPad can call me directly. You'll notice that when You try to unlock the iPad, you'll be prompted to enter a passcode. If you tap "Cancel", there's really nothing else you'll be able do with this iPad at this point. Without the passcode you can't get into it. Now if your iPad happens to be turned off at the time you send the message, the message will still appear the next time the iPad is turned on.

So, if some honest stranger picks it up and turns it on, they'll see your message and hopefully call you. Now a new feature of iOS 7 is something called "Activation Lock". In previous versions of iOS, even if you set your device as lost and remotely added a passcode. Whoever found or took your device could connect it to a computer and iTunes and completely erase the iPad and pop in a new SIM card. It would be impossible to find using "Find My iPad". With iOS 7 installed in your device however, anyone who takes your iPad can't disable "Find My iPad", can't erase it and can't restore it without knowing both your Apple ID and password.

Apple's been spreading the word about "Activation Lock" fairly well and as more people become aware of it. I think it's becoming clear that there's very little incentive to steal an iOS device since you can't just wipe it clean without a username and password.

Finally, the last button is "Erase iPad". This is for when you've pretty much exhausted all your options and you just want to make sure that whoever found or stole your device can't get to any of the data stored on it. Just click "Erase iPad". And you'll see this message telling you that this will erase all of your settings and data, and that you'll no longer be able to track your iPad. Also be aware that this can't be undone.

So if you're sure you want or need to do this, you can click "Erase", and you'll be prompted to enter your Apple ID's password. Now the semi-good news is, even after you've wiped your iPad, if you happen to find it or it gets returned to you. you can still sync it to your computer again. The back up that was created the last time you synced will be copied back to your iPad. Now it's also worth mentioning here that if you have more than one iOS device, you might want to download the free app called Find My iPad/Find my iphone. This is an app from Apple that offers the same services available through the iCloud website, but it's offered in handy app form.

Just to make sure "Find My iPad" is turned on under Settings> iCloud, and again just make sure the "Find My iPad" switch is on. Then on any iPhone, iPad, or iPod Touch on which you've installed the app, start the app. Enter your Apple ID and password, and then you'll see a list of all the iPhones, iPads, iPod Touches, and Macs registered to your iCloud account. Just tap one of your devices to see its location on a map. In the upper right-hand corner, you can tap the car icon to open up the Maps app and get driving directions to where your device is located.

At the bottom of the screen tap Actions and you'll find the same features we just looked at on the iCloud site for playing a sound, putting the device into lost mode, or erasing the device. So as you can see, you get the same functionality in this app as you do on the iCloud website. But this is a nicer interface to use when you're on an iPad and it's a free app so it's worth downloading on your devices, if you have more than one iOS device. Of course if you only have one iPad, there's no point in installing the app since if you lose your iPad, it obviously won't matter if the app is installed on it or not. Okay, so that's a rundown of the services available from "Find My iPad", which again is part of the free iCloud collection of online services from Apple.

Child Proofing the iPad

Those of you who have an iPad and kids already know this. For those of you who don't, let me tell you. The iPad is a kid magnet; they love the thing. But it's an unwise parent who lets them lay their hands on the iPad without first doing a little work to ensure the safety of your child's sensibilities, as well as your wallet. Here are some tips for childproofing your iPad. Launch "Settings", tap "General", and then tap "Restrictions".

Tap "Enable Restrictions" and then enter and verify a passcode. The "Restrictions" options will then become available to you. Anytime you or someone else attempts to modify "Restrictions" settings, they'll be prompted for this passcode.

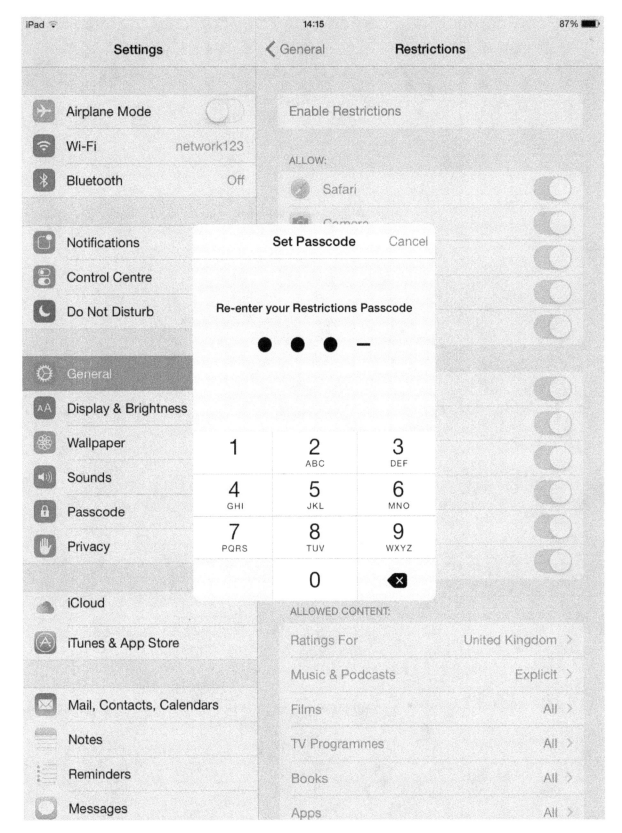

In the app area near the top of the screen, you can switch on or off Safari, YouTube, Camera, FaceTime, iTunes, and iTunes's Ping social networking service. You can also disallow installing and deleting apps. To disallow any of these options, you just flick the toggle switches to off. If you don't want your kid accessing the Internet, switch off Safari and YouTube. You might also want to turn off FaceTime so that they can't communicate with others.

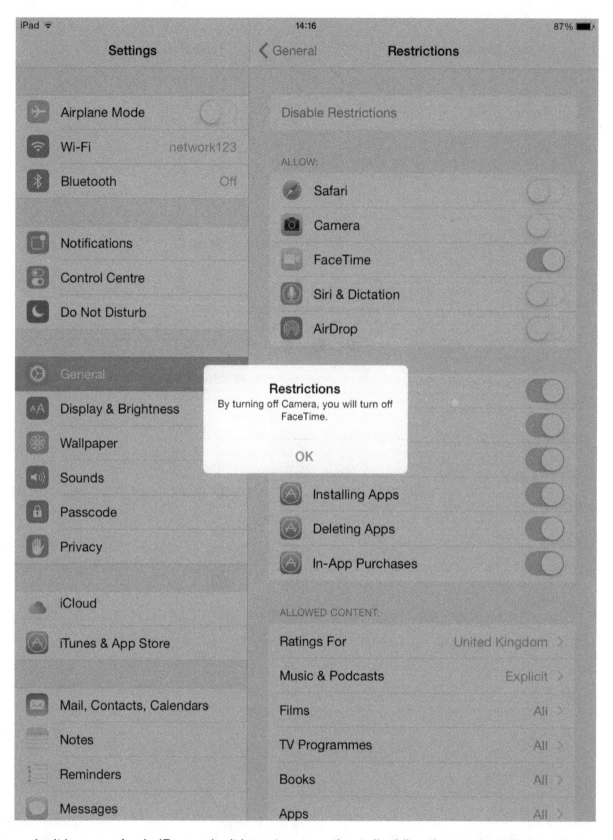

If you don't have an Apple ID, you don't have to worry about disabling the app installations, but you might want to keep your moody teenager from deleting apps, particularly if you have had them performing some onerous chores lately. Now let's look at "Locations". You can also disallow any apps from using "Location services" or just the specific apps you choose.

Tap "Location" and you'll see a list of all the apps on your iPad that use "Location". I'd be wary about any app that broadcasts to the world where a child might be, lock down the Camera app too.

Also lock down any social networking apps, such as Twitter and Facebook. If you don't want to be choosy, you can flick the Location services switch to OFF, and then the iPad can't use "Location" until you later turn it back ON.

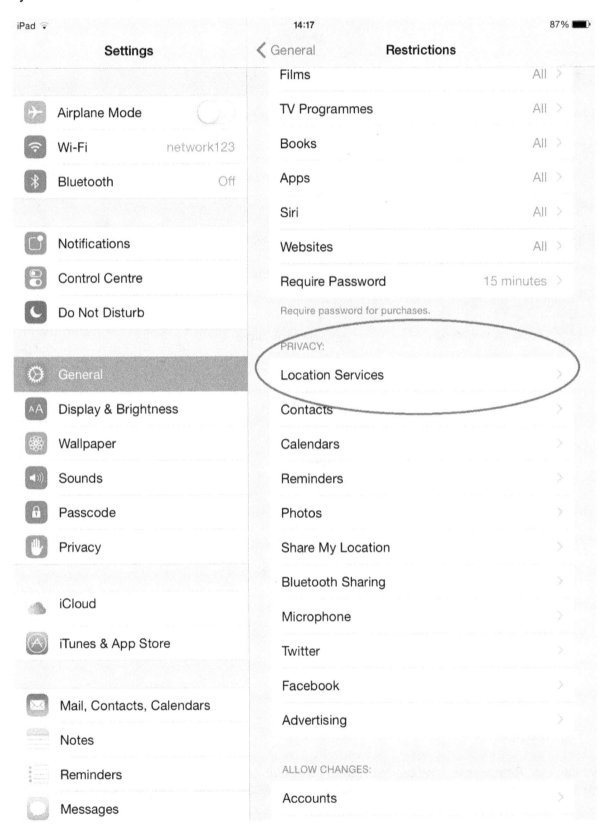

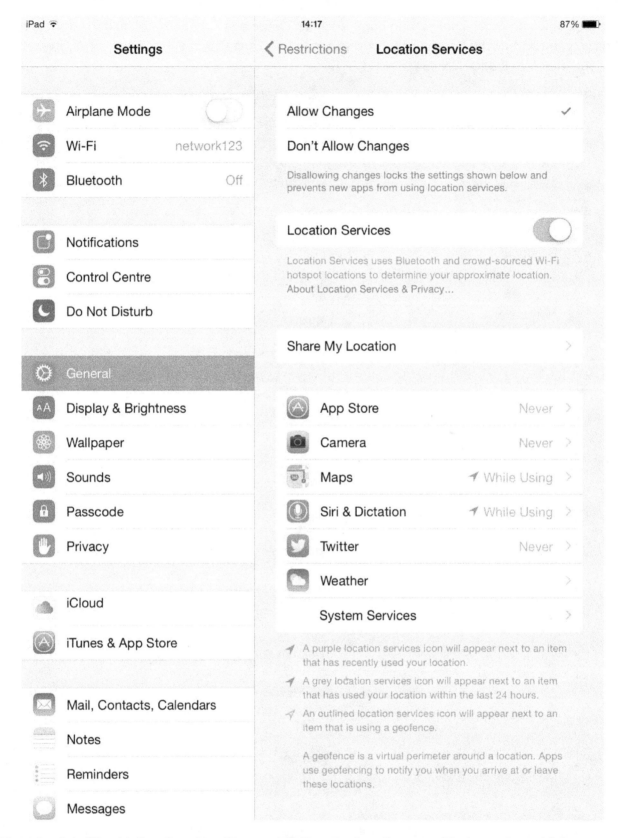

Move back to "Restrictions" and tap "Accounts". If you're handing your iPad over to a child, you might also want to disallow the ability to make changes to your "Mail, Contacts, and Calendars" accounts. Do this by tapping "Accounts", and then "Don't Allow Changes".

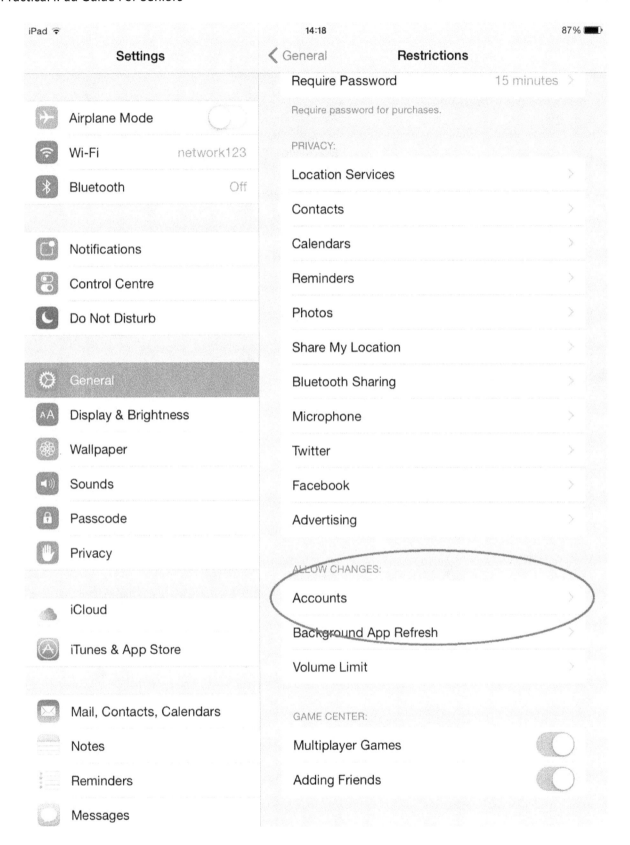

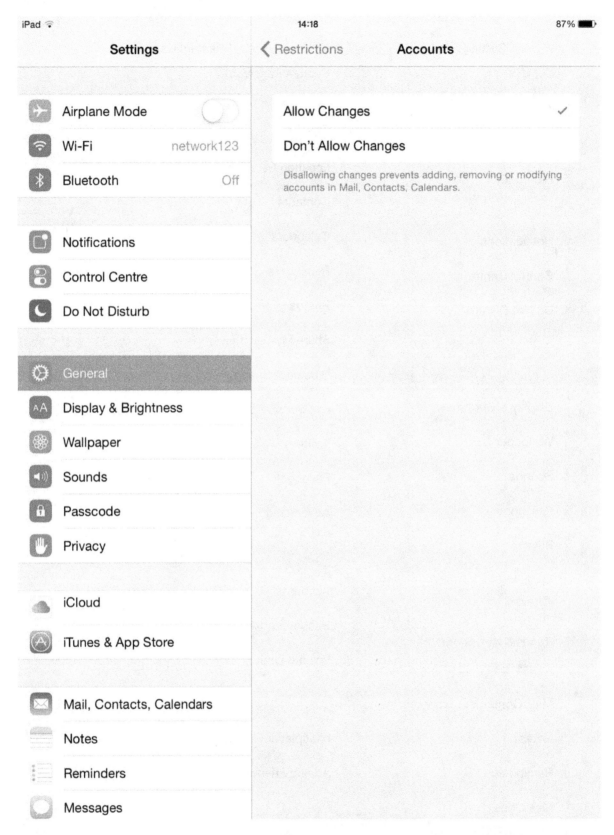

The "Allowed Content" area exists so that you can control your iPad's media. For example, you can disallow "In-app Purchases", which can be a good thing, as many of these things are tempting and they can add up. You can then filter what your child can see by choosing "Ratings". For instance, tap "Music & Podcasts" and you can keep kids from listening to content that's marked EXPLICIT.

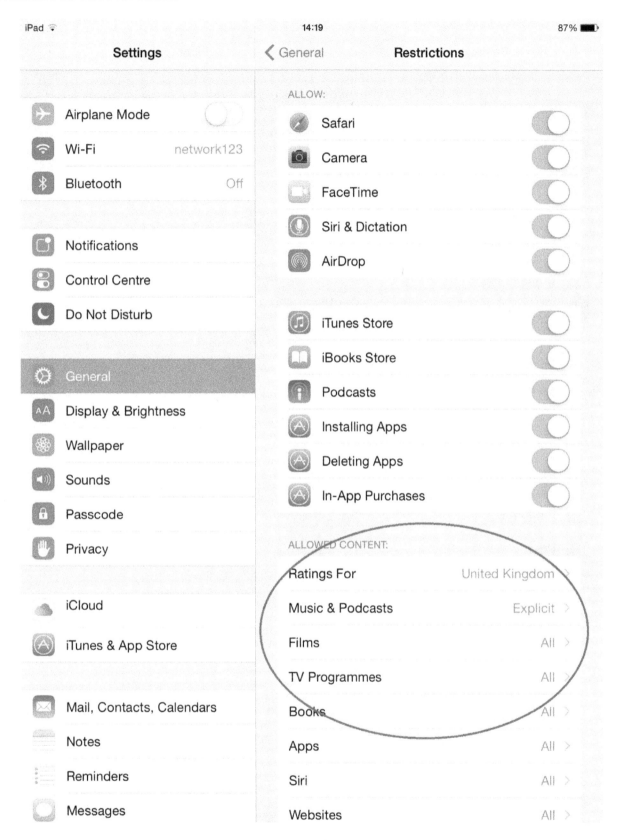

Likewise, you can allow your kid to watch G- and PG-rated movies, but not PG-13, R, and NC-17 films. So all you have to do is tap PG and the other ratings are disabled. Or you can go whole hog and tap "Don't Allow Movies". This "Don't Allow at all" setting is particularly helpful if the TV shows and movies you have on your iPad weren't obtained from the iTunes Store. Movies you've obtained elsewhere don't have a rating code embedded in them, and so the iPad can't tell whether they're rated G or NC-17.

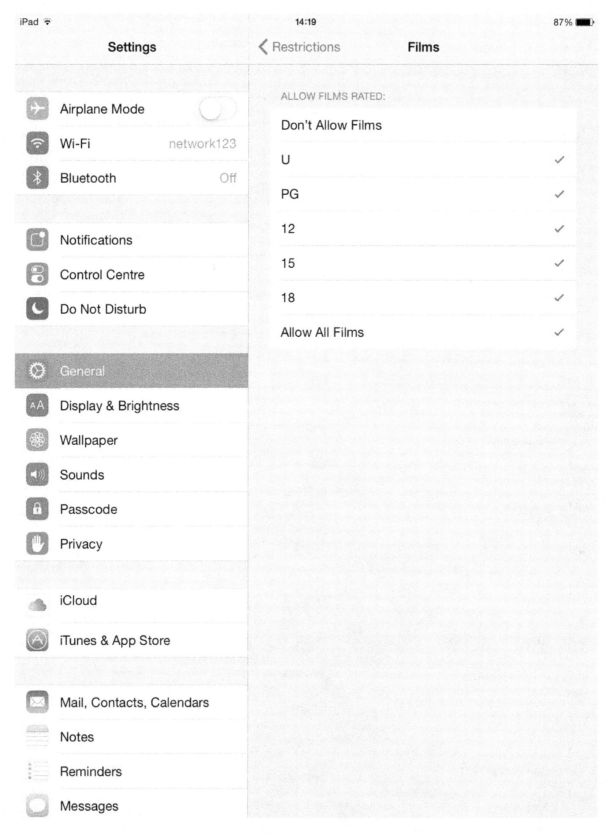

If you turn off the ability to watch any movies and TV shows, you needn't be concerned about this. You can do the same kind of thing with TV Shows. So, for example, if you only want things rated TV-G and below, simply tap that rating and the higher- rated shows are now disabled. Apps are rated as well, by age rather than rating. Apple's ratings air on the side of safety, so you can trust that when you choose 4+, your child will be able to use only the most tame apps.

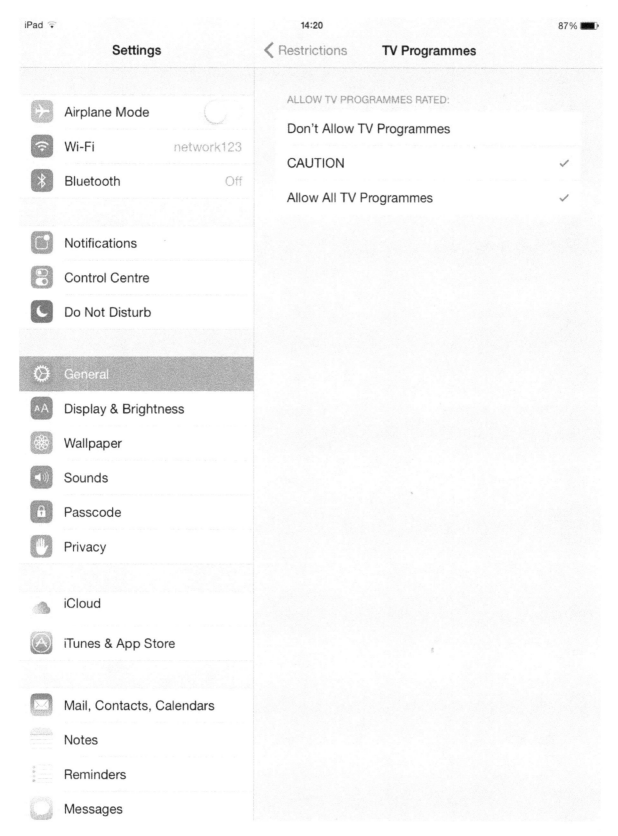

And finally, there are "Game Center Restrictions". In this regard, you only need to know that it's Apple's social networking service that allows registered players to compare scores and mark game achievements. If you prefer that your child does not participate in multiplayer games, as they sometimes allow players to chat with each other, you can turn off the "Multiplayer Games" option. You can also switch off the option to "Add Friends to Game Center", which is a good idea if it's your iPad and you don't want a bunch of 12-year-olds telling you what a lame Angry Birds player you are.

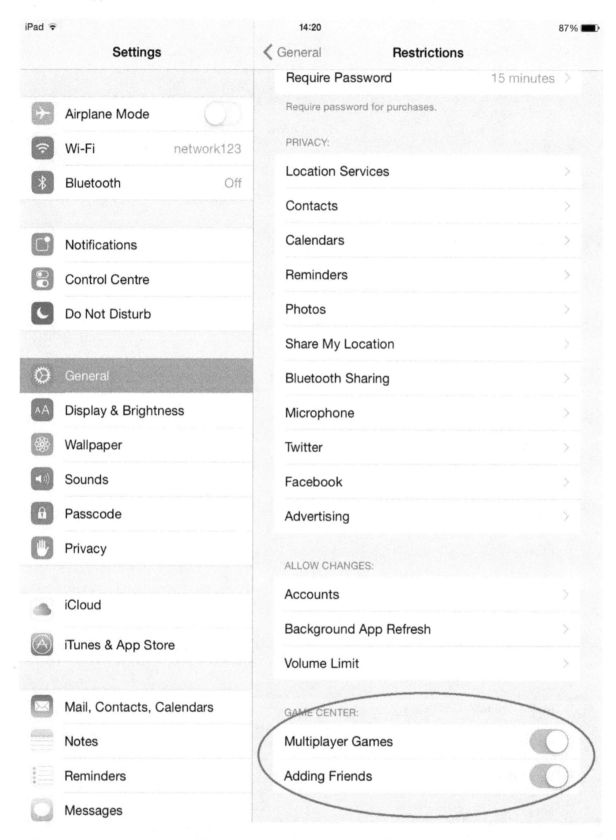

Now these are the restrictions built into the iPad, but there are some other things that you can do to help protect your child. If you don't want your kid to switch on an R-rated movie when she's using the iPad on a long car trip, don't put that movie on the iPad. Likewise, in that long-car-trip scenario, sync the iPad only with age-appropriate apps. Secondly, do not give a child the password for your Apple ID. If you want an app, look at it first, and then you buy it without your child looking on, as you type your password. Check games that include social networking options where a stranger could chat with your younger child. Some very innocent-looking games have such options, and it takes only one creep to ruin your and your child's day.

If such options exist, look for a way to switch them off and talk to your child about why you need to do this. Unlike with your computer, there are no ways to fine-tune where your child can go on the Internet. If you're not ready to have your child exposed to the big bad Internet, be sure to browse with them. Or as we've done here, switch off Safari using "Restrictions". And finally, talk to your child about what is and isn't appropriate to do with your iPad. This includes not only the kinds of apps and content they're allowed to view, but also the amount of time that they spend on it.

The iPad may be one of the coolest toys on earth, but it's no replacement for being with real, live people and spending time engaged in healthy pursuits.

Accessibility Settings

Strange as it may seem for a device that lacks a physical keyboard and pointing device, the iPad is quite accessible to those with disabilities. It is because Apple is at the forefront of making devices that can be used by everyone. But the iPad's accessibility features aren't useful only to those with vision and hearing problems. Those without such issues can use some of these features as well. However, there's an obvious question and that is, if you can't see well, how can you possibly navigate the iPad in order to get to its accessibility features? And the answer is through iTunes on your computer.

If you have vision issues and are using a computer, it's likely you have it configured so that you can navigate around it, by using Apple's VoiceOver technology on your Mac. So launch iTunes and select the iPad in iTunes's source list. In the Summary pane, scroll down to the bottom and click "Configure Universal Access". Switch on VoiceOver, click OK, and Continue, then move to the iPad. With VoiceOver engaged, you can now move about the iPad by touching the iPad and listening to spoken navigational commands.

You can use VoiceOver to navigate to the Accessibility feature. Drag your finger until you locate and highlight the "Settings" app, and then launch "Settings" just by double-tapping somewhere on the screen. You need to be in the "Settings" window, and the "General" setting should be highlighted.

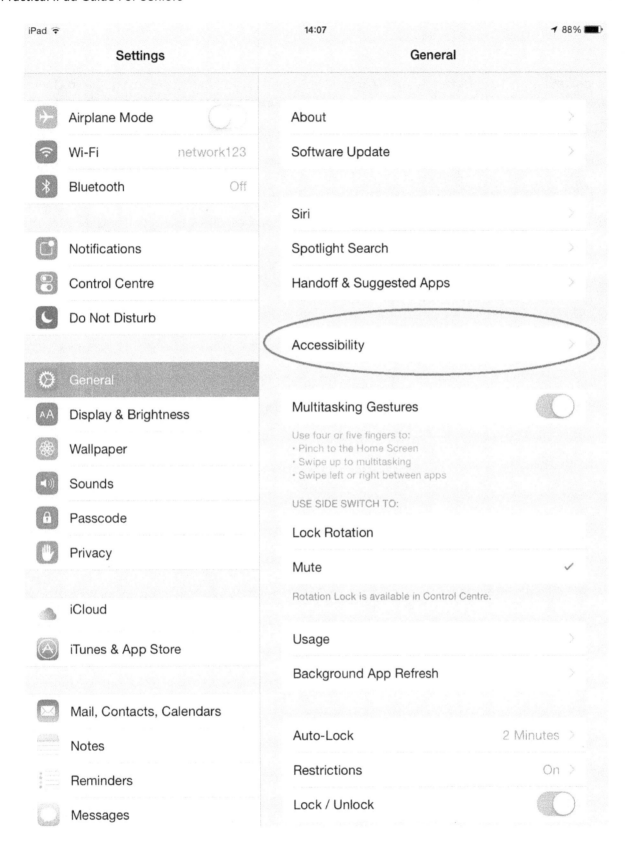

If it isn't, move your finger until Voiceover directs you to "General". Double tap when you find it. Next you'll need to tap and drag with three fingers to scroll down the window, in order to find the "Accessibility" option. When you find it, double tap again.

You can zoom in and out by dragging three fingers around the screen. Drag them down the screen to make it smaller and up to make it larger.

Let's look at Large Text. Select "Large Text" and you see that you can make text larger in Contacts, Mail, and Notes.

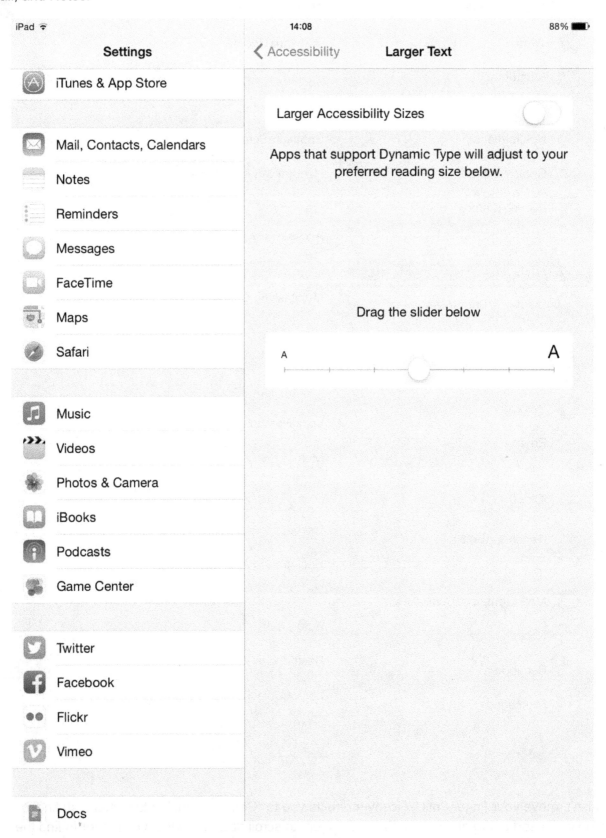

You can also increase the contrast of everything on the screen to help you if you are visually challenged.

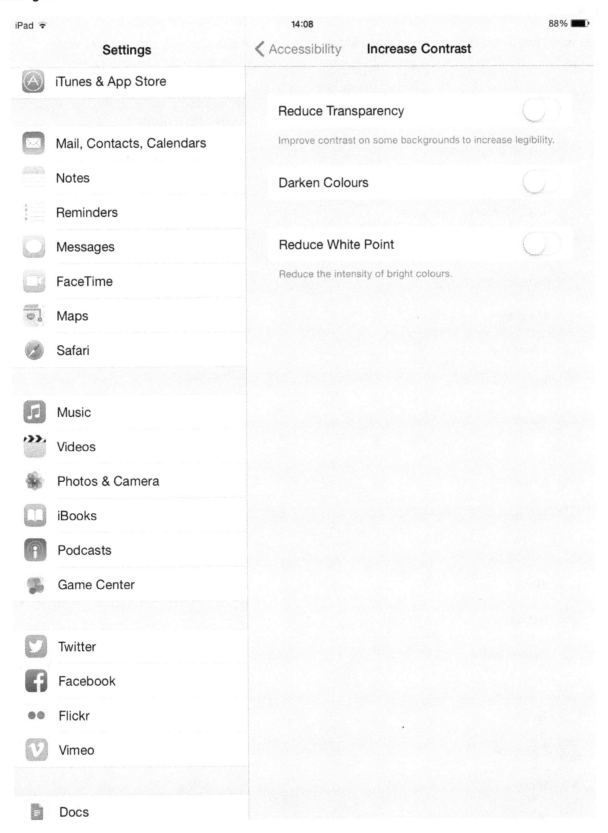

Now how is this useful? Well, people who have vision problems find higher contrast easier to read in some cases, but it can also be used by people who don't have vision problems. For example, if you like to read in bed at night and the person you're sleeping with really resents the fact that there's this really bright light in the background when you're reading a book, even though you can adjust the brightness on the thing, you may want to turn this on. The text is still very legible, but you don't have that bright shine coming out of the iPad as you would if you had the iPad set to its normal setting.

If you need some assistance when watching videos on your device, you can request video descriptions, which will provide you with spoken descriptions of the action on the screen.

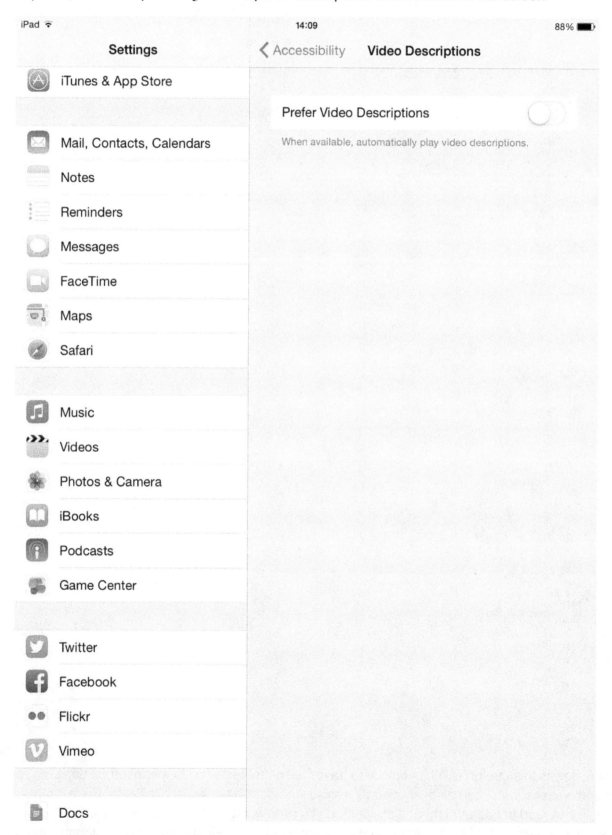

If you wear wireless hearing aids, that are compatible with bluetooth, you simple need to switch both your hearing aids and your bluetooth on, in order to benefit from them.

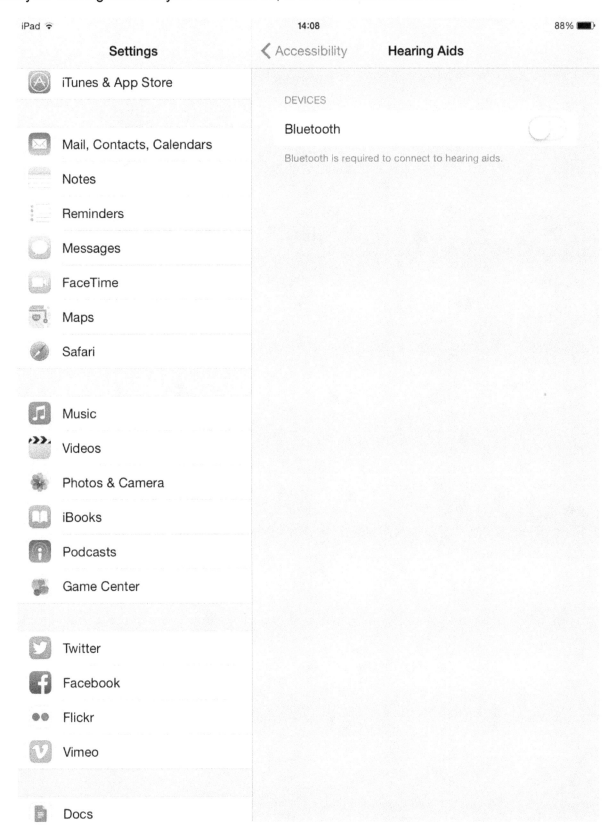

Speak Auto-text is another useful feature of "Accessibility". The iPad will speak any auto-correction it makes, making it easier to notice, and if necessary, to correct.

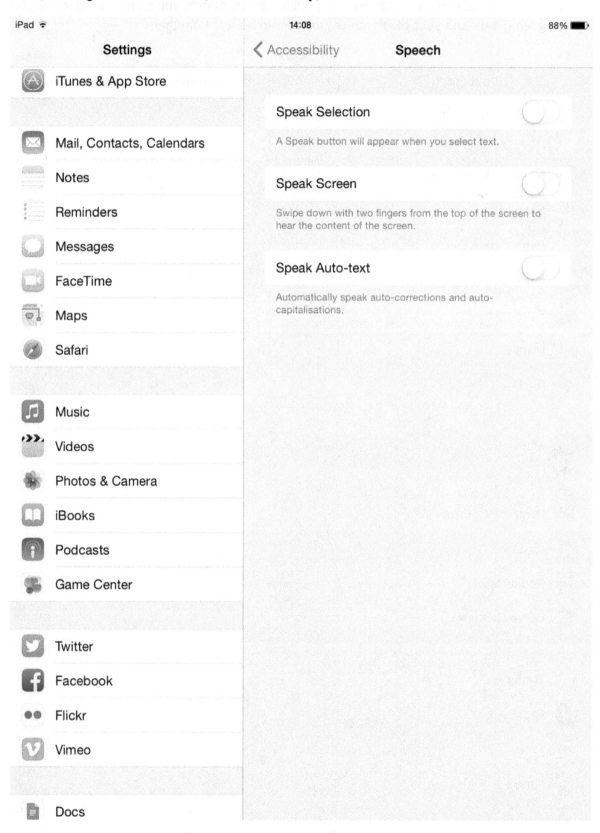

If you have trouble touching the screen in order to use any of standard finger gestures outlined in this book, it's perfectly possible to create a new finger gesture, that suits both your physical capabilities and what you wish to achieve on your device. Assistive touch will allow you to create the unique gesture.

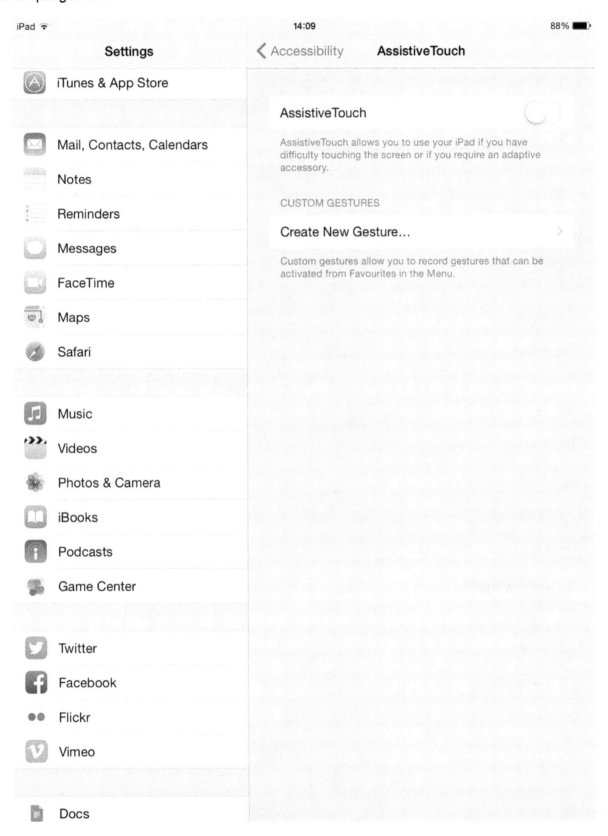

And last, there is the Triple-click Home button option. Tap it and you'll find that you can configure a triple-click of the Home button to perform one of the iPad's accessibility tricks, Guided Access. Guided Access limits the screen to enable users to focus on one task at a time, without getting distracted. This is particularly useful for teachers who want to want to keep their students' mind on what they should be doing, rather than being tempted to press every other button on the device.

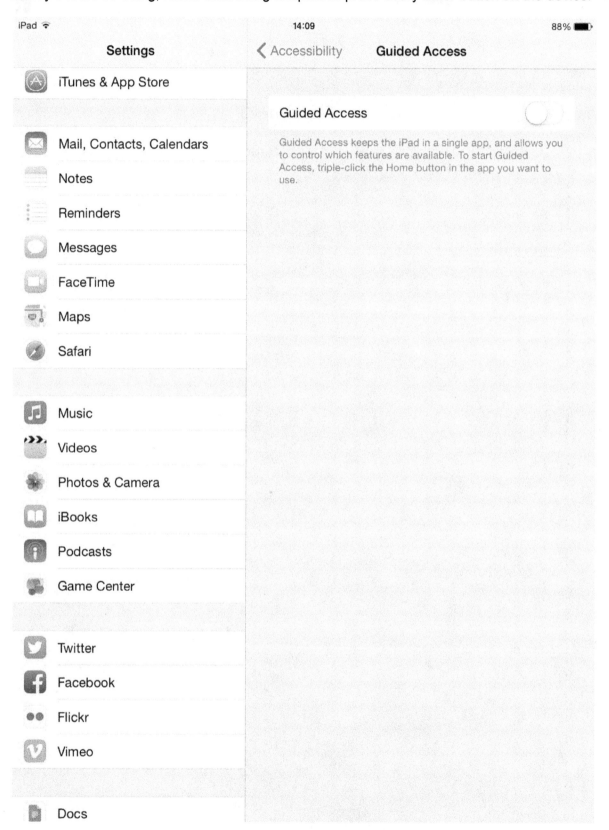

Advanced Setup

Virtual Private Networks

Virtual Private Networks, or VPNs, allow users to connect remotely to business networks in order to access and share files, and can allow you to browse the web privately, among other tasks. To connect to a VPN, you can do it via the VPN manager. Open the Settings app, tap on General, then "VPN not configured", then add "VPN configuration"

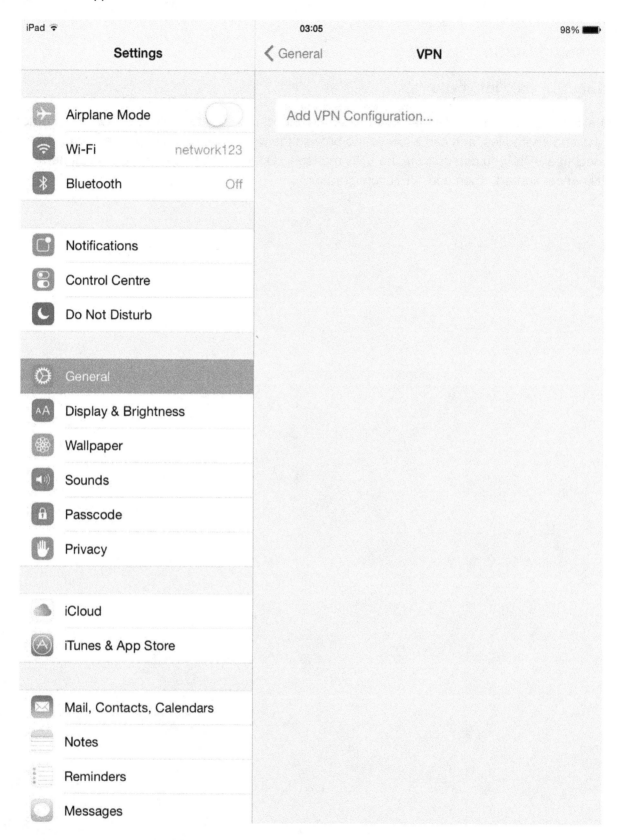

From here, you can add a VPN connection. You will need to obtain all of these details from the people who run your VPN in order to set it up correctly. Let me give you an example. Supposing you use a free VPN from justfreevpn.com, which uses the connection type "PPTP". All you'll need to do is enter a description, the server address (which will be in the format of a web address), as well as an account, which will be your username, and a password. Press save. Your VPN configuration will appear so all you have to do is turn your VPN from off to on.

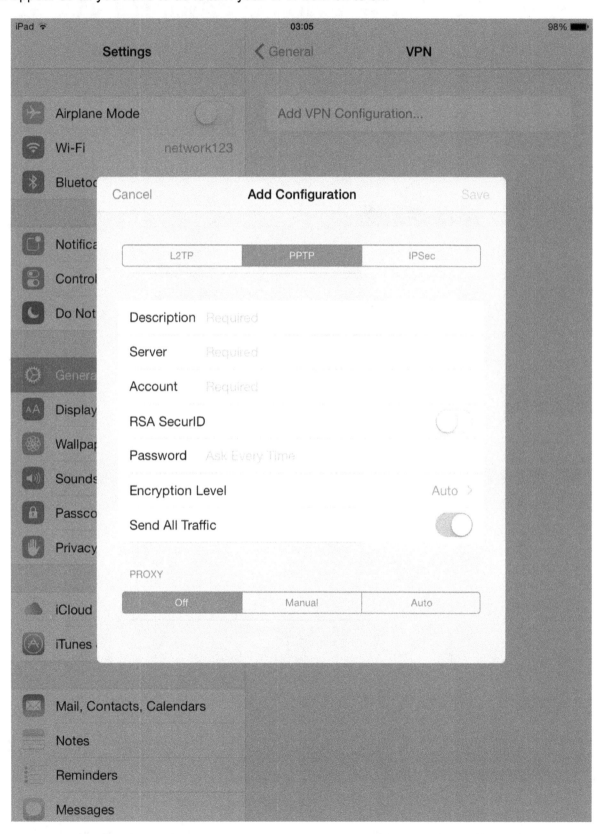

The other settings are optional and will, again, depend on what the network you are connecting to requires. Some VPNs require proxy settings, which you can configure at the bottom of the above screen. If you're using the L2TP connection, you will follow a similar prompt to input your details, but with the addition of a secret passcode.

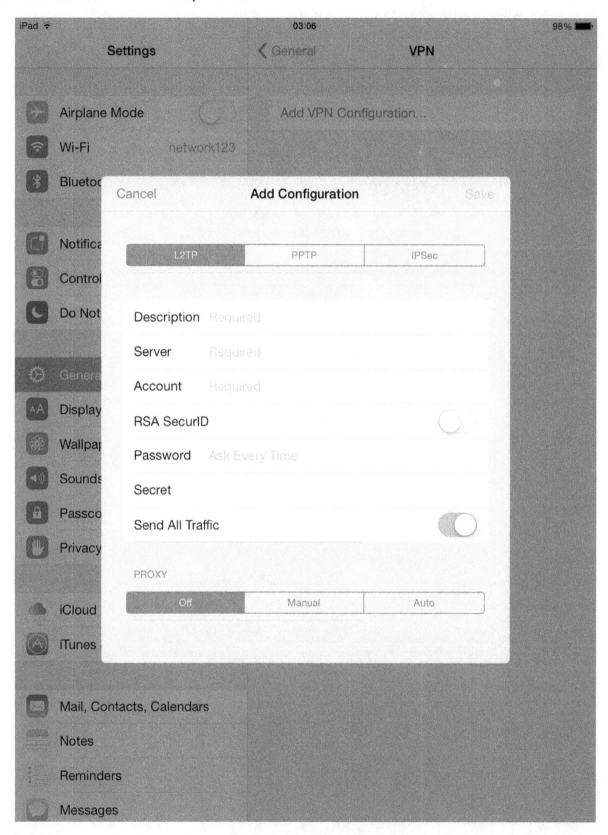

There is a third secure option and that's OpenVPN. It isn't automatically supported by ios apps, but you can download a free opensource app called OpenVPN connect, which will do the job. Bear in mind that you can add multiple VPN configurations in order to connect to different networks. To connect, select the VPN you want to connect to, then turn the VPN switch to ON. An activity indicator will appear to let you know that it is connecting. The status will change when you are connected, letting you know how long you have been connected to the network.

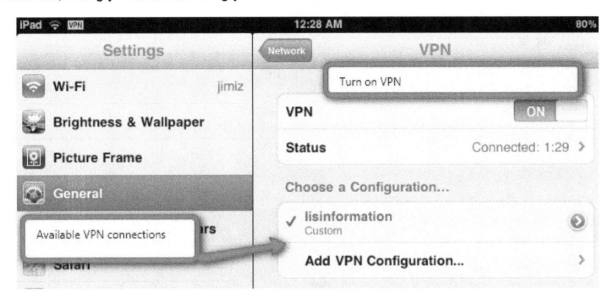

In the top left there will be an icon that lets you know you are connected to a VPN. If you want to disconnect, go to the VPN settings again, and turn the switch off. The iPad will disconnect, and you will be connecting to the internet through your normal connection.

If you wish to remove a VPN configuration, tap on the blue arrow next to its name, scroll down in the window, tap the red delete button, then on 'delete'.

The configuration will then be permanently removed from your iPad.

Privacy Settings

Apps can make requests to use your location, social accounts, and other data that you have on your iPad. These requests mean that apps can share things to twitter and Facebook, integrate with your calendar, use your photos for certain features, and more, which can enhance the experience you receive.

If you decide that you don't want an app to have certain permissions, you can revoke their access. To do this, open the Settings app, then tap on Privacy. From here, you will see a list of things that applications can request access to.

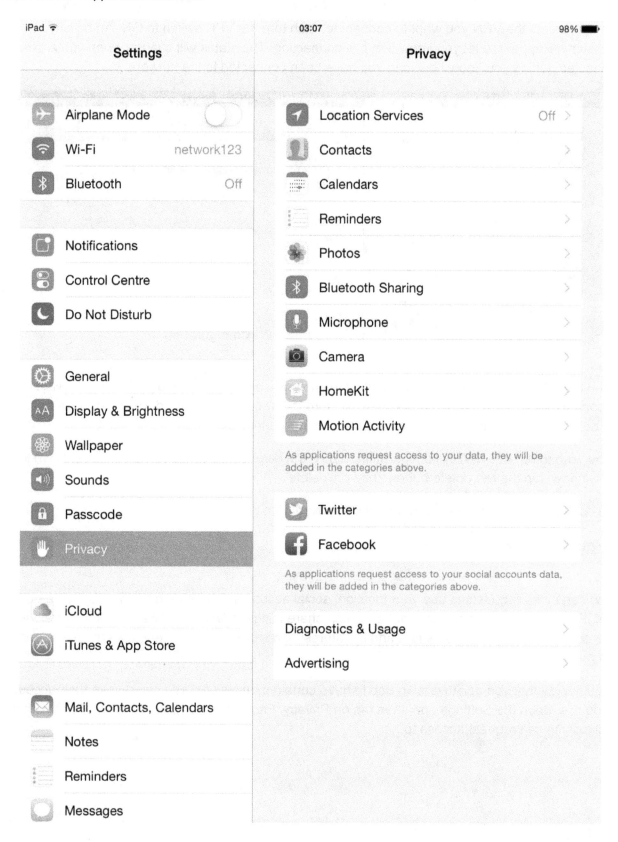

For example, an app such as Evernote may request to use your photos in order to insert them into your notes. If you decide you no longer require this service, you can tap on Photos and turn the switch to off.

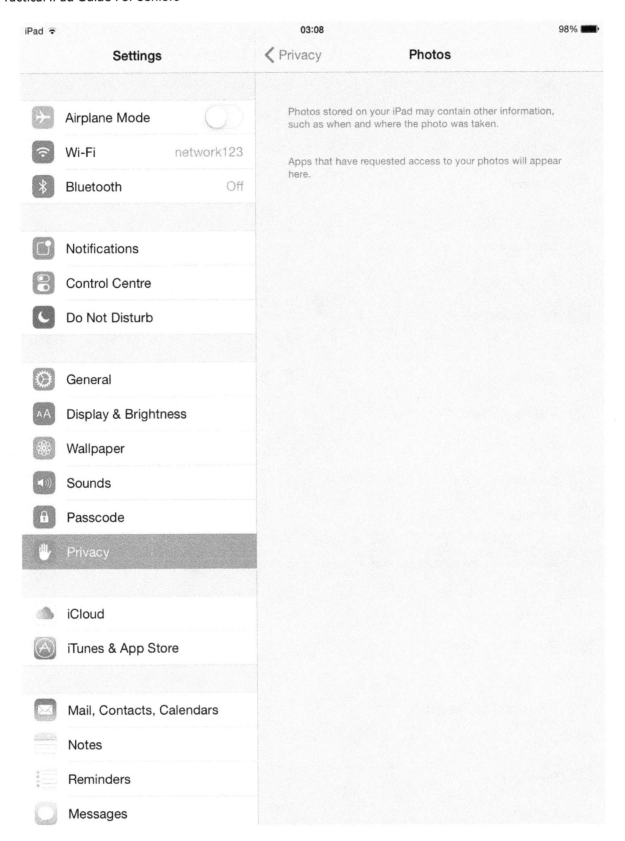

Some apps want to find out where you are. Go into "settings", then "privacy", then "location services", to find out which ones they are. If you'd rather these apps didn't know where you are, you then need to tap on "system services" on the same screen and switch off the "location based iAds".

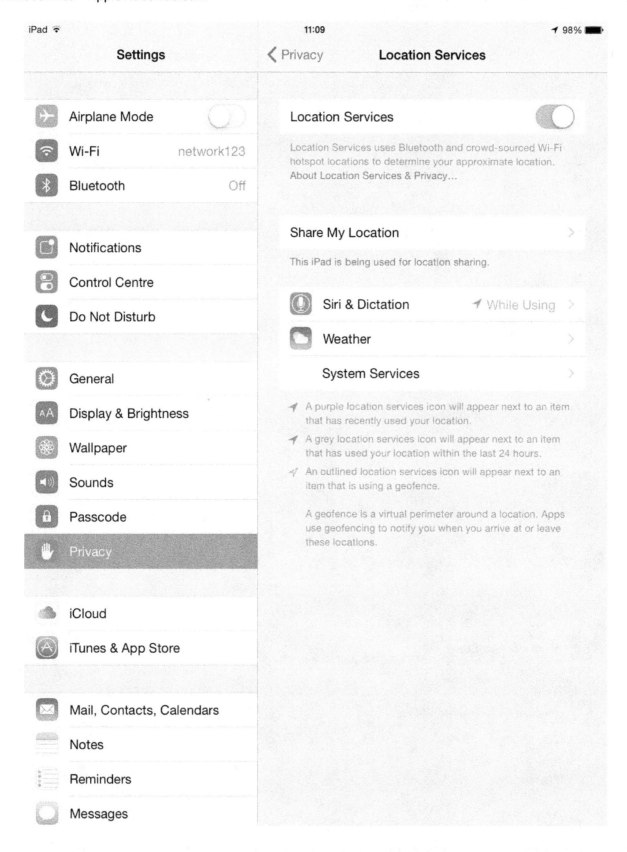

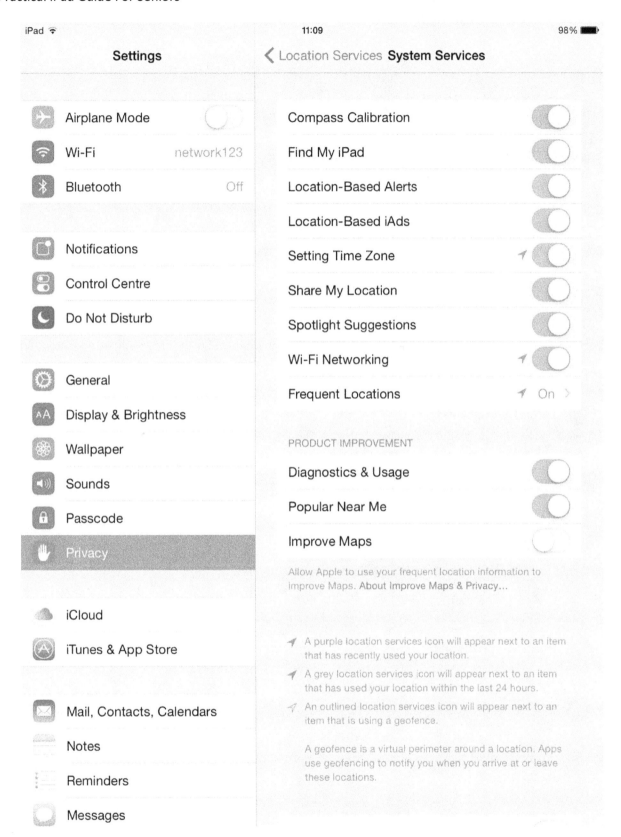

Whilst still on this screen you might also want to switch off "frequent locations", which does something similar.

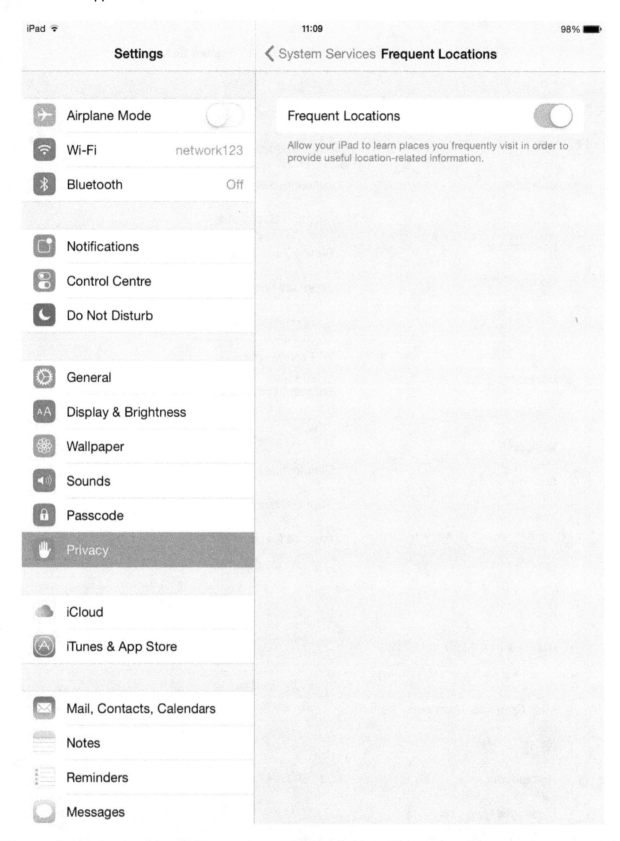

"Diagnostics and usage" is another one to consider switching off, because this app informs Apple of every action you make on your phone. And that's with your permission, unless you switch it off! This process can be repeated for all the other types of things applications have access to, including Twitter and Facebook.

If you denied an application access to something, and later find you require the service it provides, you can turn the switch to ON and the application will then be able to access that data or service.

Finally you might want to limit how much advertisers can find out about you. To do this, go into "settings", then "privacy", then "advertising". Here, switch on "limit ad tracking."

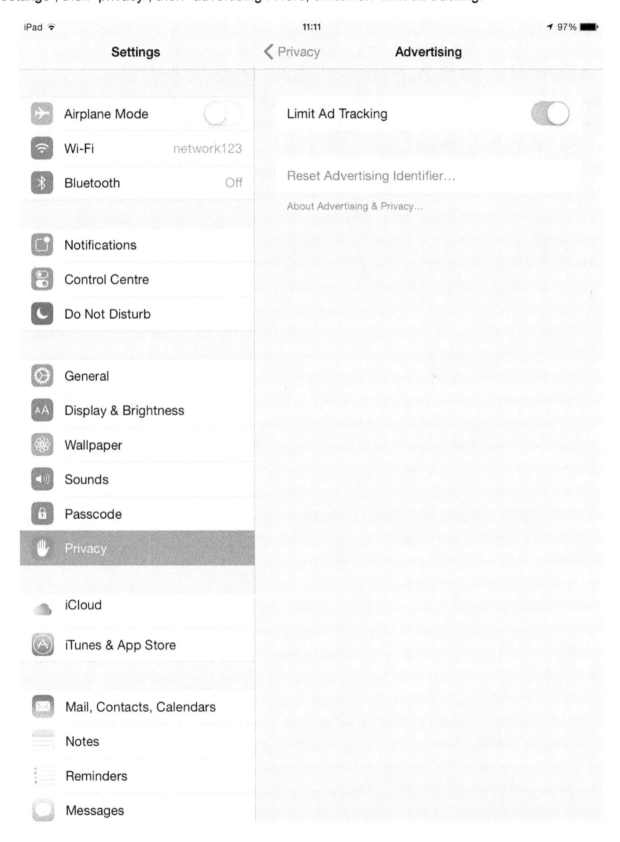

Notifications

Applications can send you notifications to let you know that something is happening which requires your attention. For example, Mail will notify you of new emails, Reminders will let you know when there's something you need to do, and Calendar tells you about upcoming events.

When you receive a notification, it will either show up as a banner at the top (which will disappear after a few seconds), or as an alert (which you have to dismiss to get rid of). Application icons can also show Badges, which display a number relevant to how many notifications or tasks you have to do in that app.

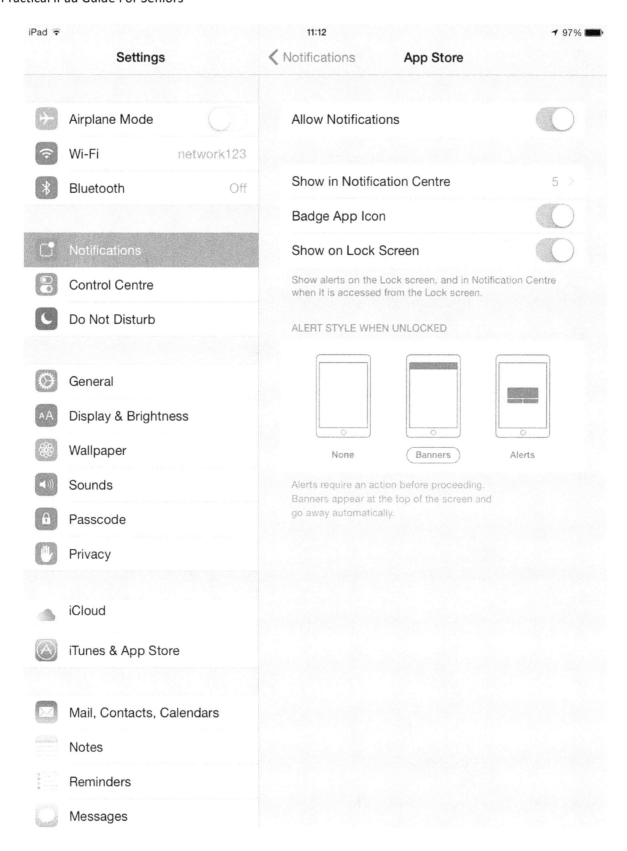

If the iPad is locked, the screen will light up for a few seconds and possibly make a sound. From the lock screen, you can see all the notifications your iPad has received since you locked it. If you want to see all your unread notifications, swipe down from the top of the screen when the iPad is unlocked, to reveal the Notification Centre. By default, Notification Centre will show all the notifications you have received and either haven't read or haven't dismissed.

Of course, the notifications from some apps are less important than others, and you can configure your notification settings to reflect this. Open the Settings app, then tap on Notifications.

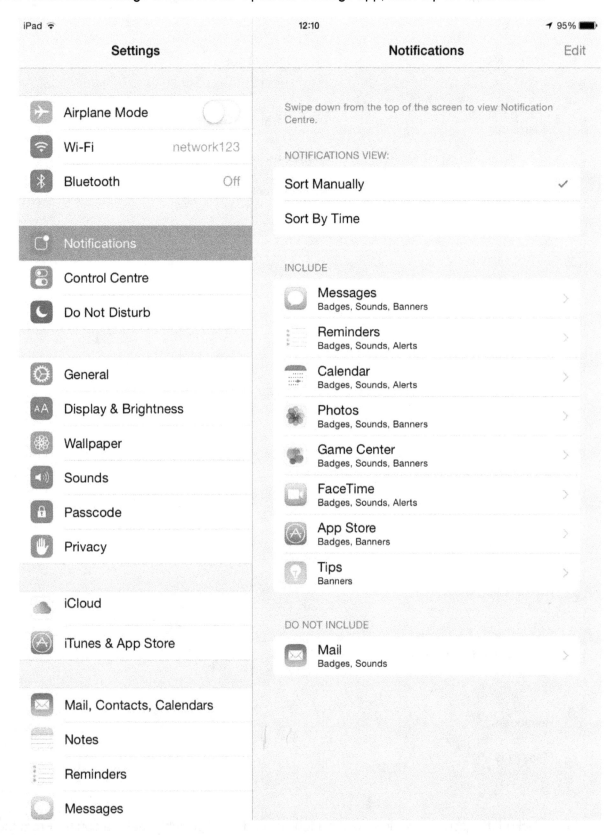

All of the applications that can send you notifications are listed in the pane.

By tapping on edit in the top right, you can drag the apps to change in which order their notifications appear in Notification Centre. If you decide you don't want to see an app's notifications in

Notification Centre, you can drag it to the very bottom, and it will no longer be displayed, although banners, alerts, and badges will still be shown. Press done when you are finished. You can also have applications automatically sorted by the time the notifications arrive.

To change what types of notifications you receive from an application, tap on its name. At the top, you can stop the app from showing notifications in Notification Centre, and change how many items it can show.

Below this, you can select the type of alert that is shown when you receive a notification. If it is not vital that you respond to an app's notification immediately, you can set it to None. This means that the app will not send you any notifications and you will have to open Notification Centre to see them. It will, however, still display badges and sounds, and show up in the Lock Screen. You can choose your notification sounds in the notification settings.

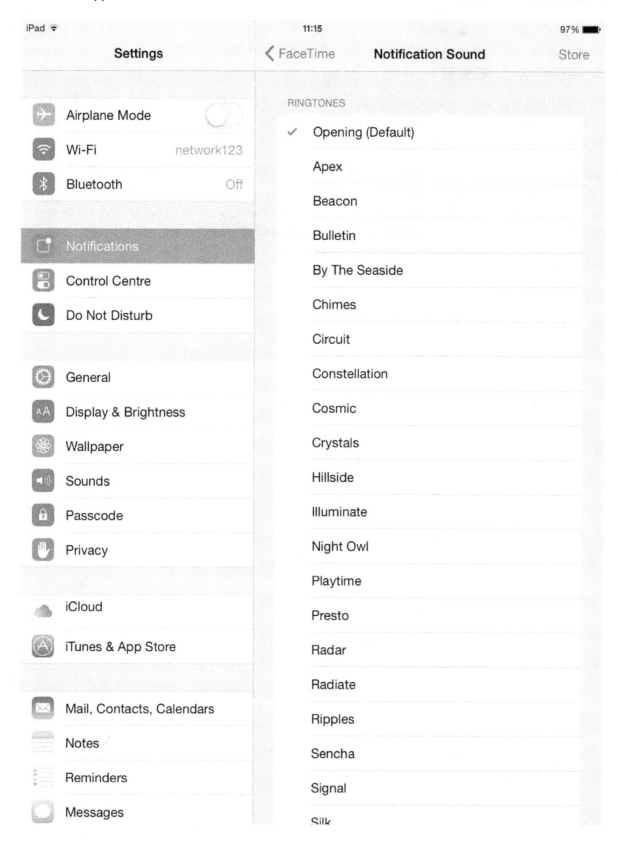

To change this, scroll down, and you will see more options. Turning off Sounds and View in Lock Screen means that the app will not bother you at all. Badges can be useful to quickly see if an app requires your attention, but if you don't want these, you can turn them off, too.

If there is an app with notifications that are somewhat important to you but do not require immediate attention, such as Tweets, Banners notifications are useful. Banners will display at the top of the screen, then disappear after a few seconds. To respond to the notification, tap on it to be taken to the app which sent it. You can also dismiss a banner notification immediately, swipe them down slightly, and then flick up.

If you have an app that sends you important notifications, you can have it send you Alert notifications. These notifications require you to either respond to the notification or to cancel it before they go away.

Mail behaves differently to other apps when it comes to notifications as you can set different preferences for each mail account. To do this, click on Mail, and then select the account you want to change the settings for. From here it is exactly the same as setting notifications for individual apps.

You can also set different notification settings for emails received from addresses you have set as VIPs, so that you will only be notified of your most important emails.

The iPad will constantly be receiving notifications when it is connected to the internet, which can be annoying at night time or if you have an important meeting in which you don't want to be disturbed. A solution this is the Do Not Disturb mode. This means that when your iPad is locked, it will not light up or make any sounds when you receive notifications.

You can activate Do Not Disturb mode manually in the Settings app, but you can also set it to be active between certain times. To do this, go to Notifications, tap on Do Not Disturb, then turn the Scheduled switch on.

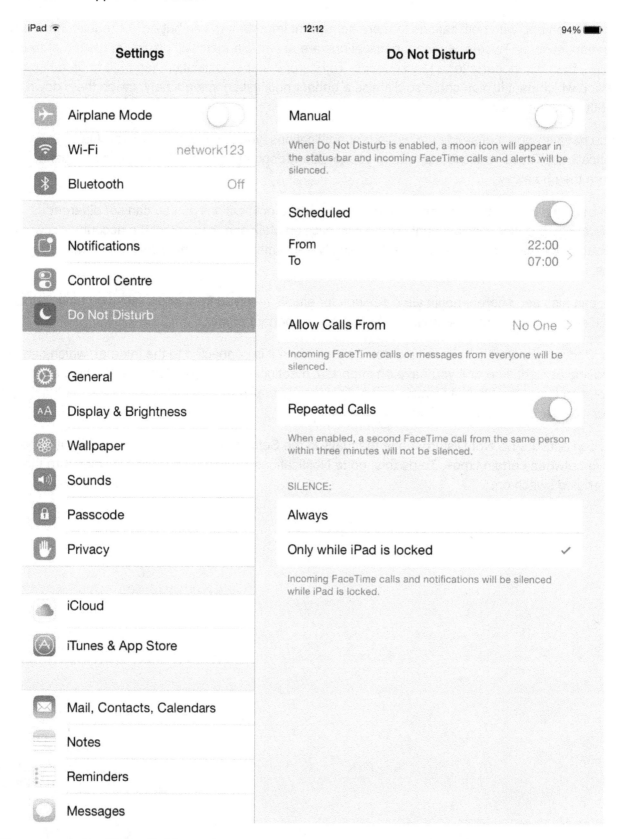

Then, tap on the "From/To" box to set the times between which you would like Do Not Disturb mode to be activated.

You can also set the iPad to notify you of FaceTime calls from people in your Favourites, certain Contact Groups, or from Everyone, even when Do Not Disturb mode is activated.

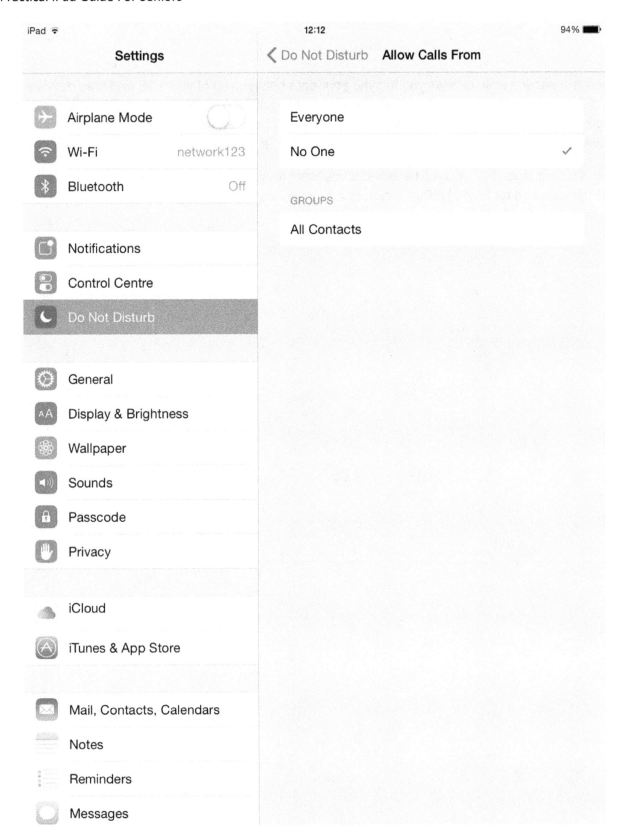

In addition to this, you can set it to notify you of multiple calls from one person within three minutes of each other. That's how to set up notifications on the iPad.

Setting up iCloud

iCloud is a service which allows you to sync your data between all of your iOS and Mac devices. If you didn't activate iCloud when you first set up your iPad, it can be done so at a later stage. To do so, go to the Settings app and tap on iCloud. If you don't have an Apple ID, or would like a new one, you can create one by tapping on "Get a Free Apple ID". If you do, enter your details here to log in.

When you are logged in, you will be asked if you want to allow iCloud to use the location of your iPad. This is used for Find My iPad, which is a free service that allows you to track and send messages to your iPad if you lose it.

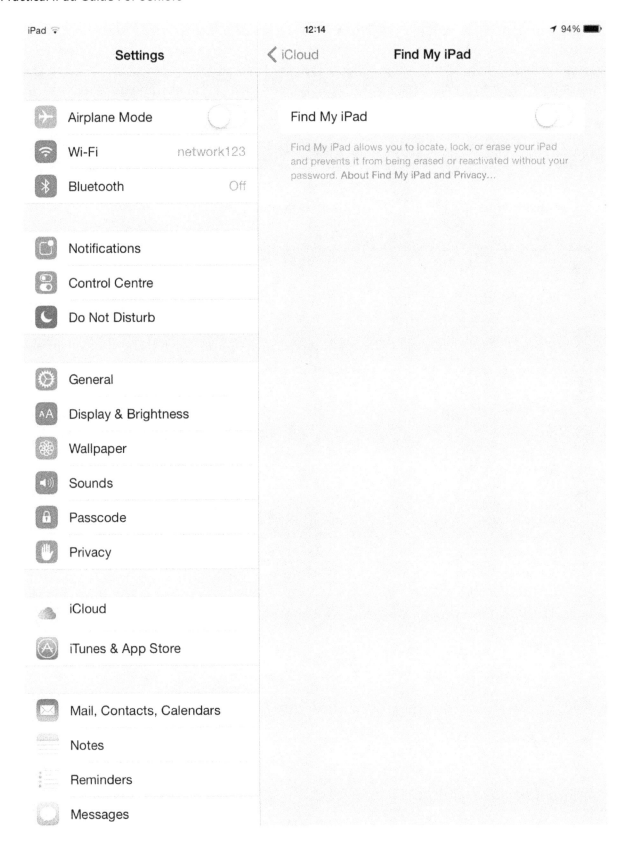

All of the options should, by default, be set to on. If you decide that you don't want to sync certain things with iCloud, you can turn the switches to off. With some options, such as Contacts, you will be asked if you would like to keep the data on your iPad or not. If you decide not to, this data can normally be retrieved by turning the switch on again.

You might also want to set up iCloud keychain. This is a security measure that keeps your passwords, credit card numbers and account names safer by encrypting them. You can enable it by going into "settings", then "iCloud", then "iCloud keychain" and switching it on or off. The first time you use it, you'll have to create a passcode. Make a brand new one to ensure you're extra secure.

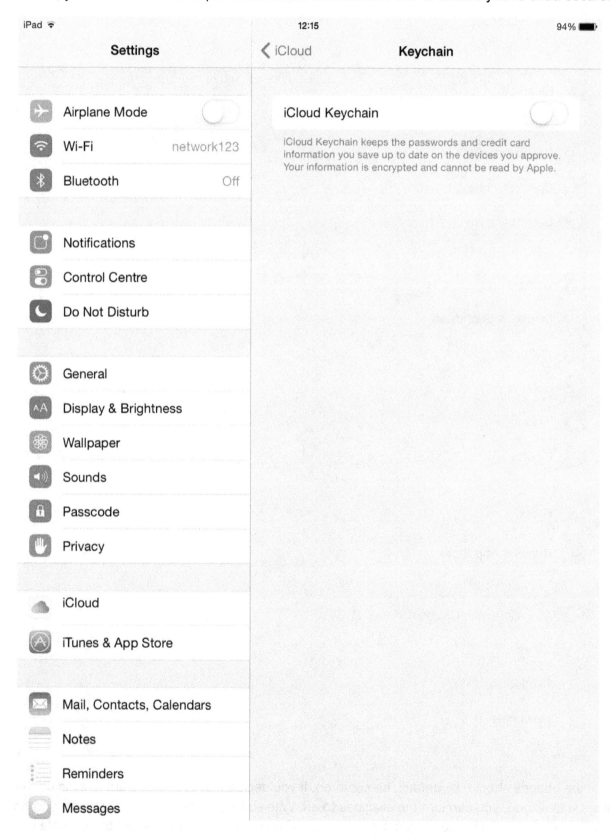

Photo Stream syncs all the photos you take between your devices. Shared Photo streams allow you to share photos with others, and can either be shared by you, or shared with you by another person. If you do not want to allow anyone to share a Photo Stream with you, turn this option off.

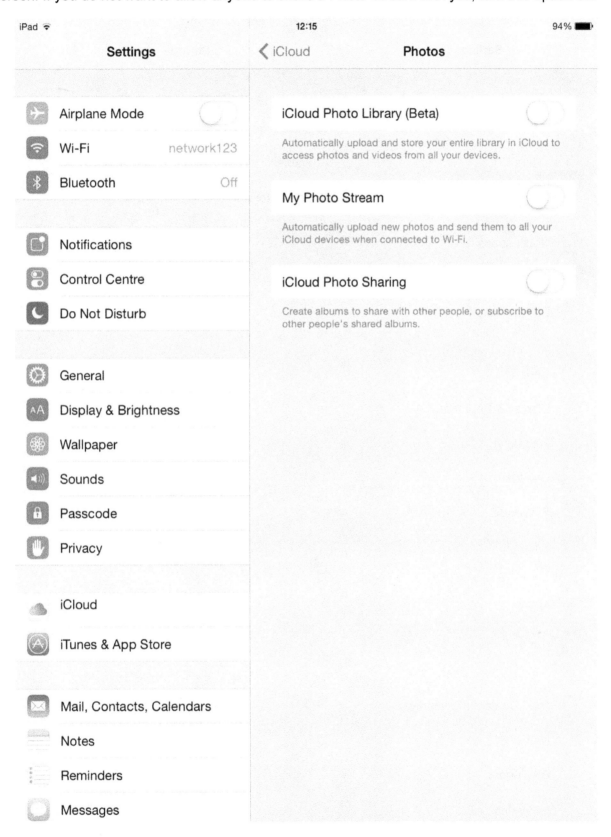

The Documents and Data setting relates to the content that apps you downloaded from the App Store are syncing via iCloud. If you do not want to allow other apps to sync data between your devices, turn this option off. At the bottom is an option for Storage and Backup.

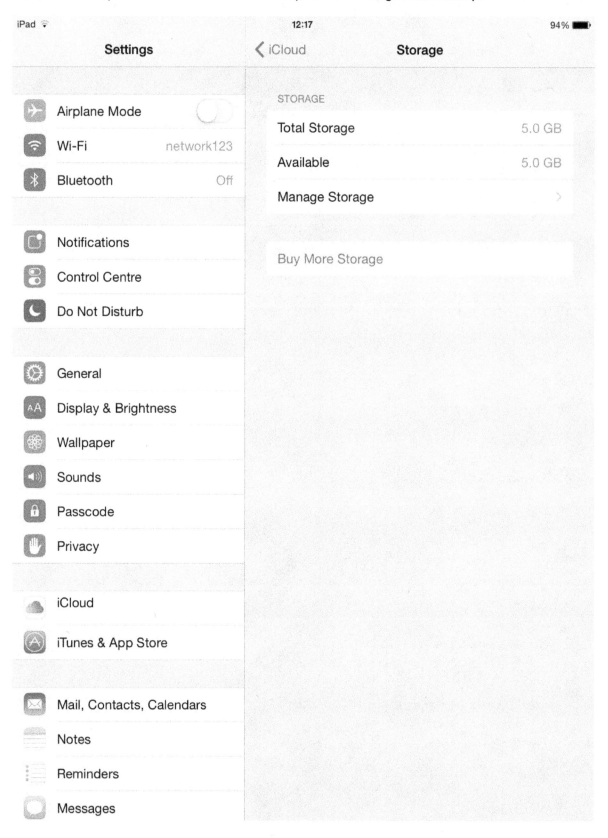

By enabling iCloud backup, your iPad will automatically update itself to the cloud every night if you connect it to the power, switch the wi-fi on and lock the screen. Make sure "iCloud backup" in settings is switched on. If your iCloud backup isn't working , it might be because your iCloud is full, or there's a problem with the email address connected to your iCloud account. It needs to be your email address and it needs to be active. There's less chance of losing your data.

Setting up Bluetooth

Bluetooth on the iPad allows you to connect to devices such as keyboards and speakers, to enhance your experience. I'm going to explain how to connect to a Bluetooth keyboard, but the process is much the same for other devices.

First, turn on the Bluetooth device. Then, open the Settings app on the iPad, and tap on Bluetooth. If it isn't already, turn the switch on. Your iPad will begin searching for devices.

iPad 📶	12:18	🧭 ᛒ 94% 🔋
Settings	**Bluetooth**	

✈️ Airplane Mode ⬜

📶 Wi-Fi   network123

ᛒ Bluetooth   On

📱 Notifications

🎛️ Control Centre

🌙 Do Not Disturb

⚙️ General

🔤 Display & Brightness

🌸 Wallpaper

🔊 Sounds

🔒 Passcode

✋ Privacy

☁️ iCloud

Ⓐ iTunes & App Store

✉️ Mail, Contacts, Calendars

📝 Notes

📋 Reminders

💬 Messages

Bluetooth   ⬜

DEVICES ⟳

When it finds the device – the names may sometimes make sense, or may seem quite odd – tap on it, and it will attempt to pair. Make sure the devices are within 10 feet of each other. Any further away and they'll be out of range of one another.

For most devices, there will be something you have to do to pair it the iPad. This keyboard requires a code to be entered in order for the pairing to complete. Once your iPad has paired with the device, it will show up as Connected, and you will be able to use it.

Now, your iPad should automatically connect whenever it is in range of the device. If you would like to stop this from happening, you can unpair the device by opening the Bluetooth settings, tapping on the blue arrow next to the device, and tapping on "Forget this Device".

If you are not using Bluetooth, it is worthwhile to turn it off, as it will save you some battery life. And that's how to set up a Bluetooth device on your iPad.

Working With Mail App

Configuring Email

Adding email accounts on the iPad is quite easy. First, open the Settings app, tap on Mail, Contacts, Calendars, then on "Add Account".

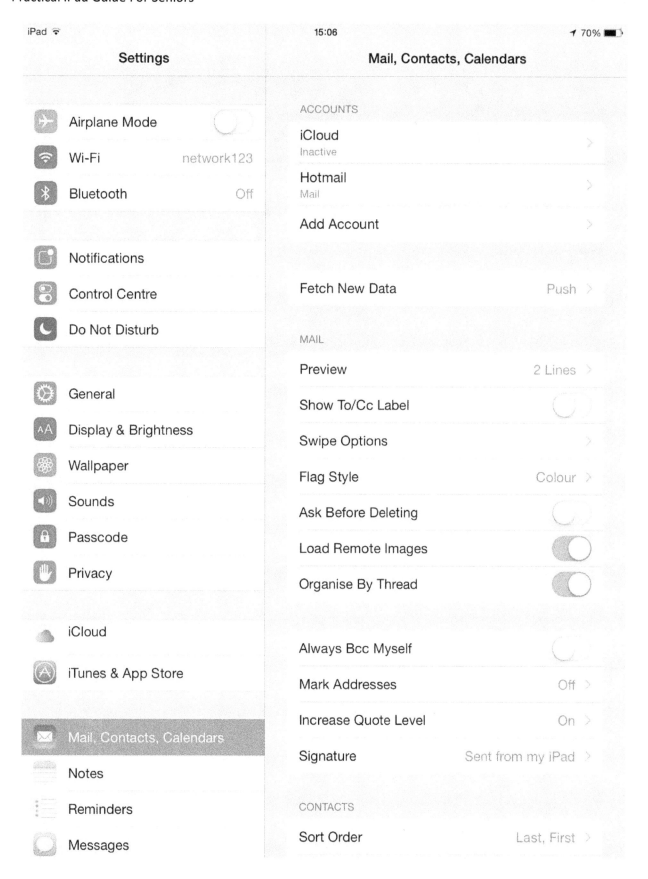

If your email is with one of the providers listed, setting up your email is as easy as typing in your name, email address and password.

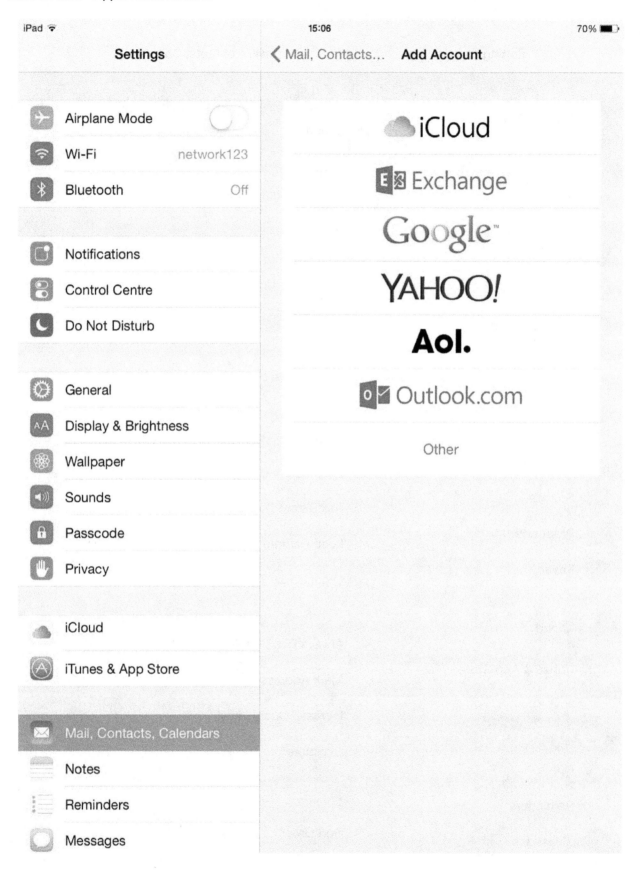

If, however, you have an email account with a different provider or if you host your own email account, there are more steps to take. First, tap on Other, then tap on "Add Mail Account". Enter your name, email address, password, and a description for the account, then tap Next. Your iPad will attempt to find the server that you need to connect to in order to receive your email. Often this will work automatically, but sometimes you will need to enter the information manually.

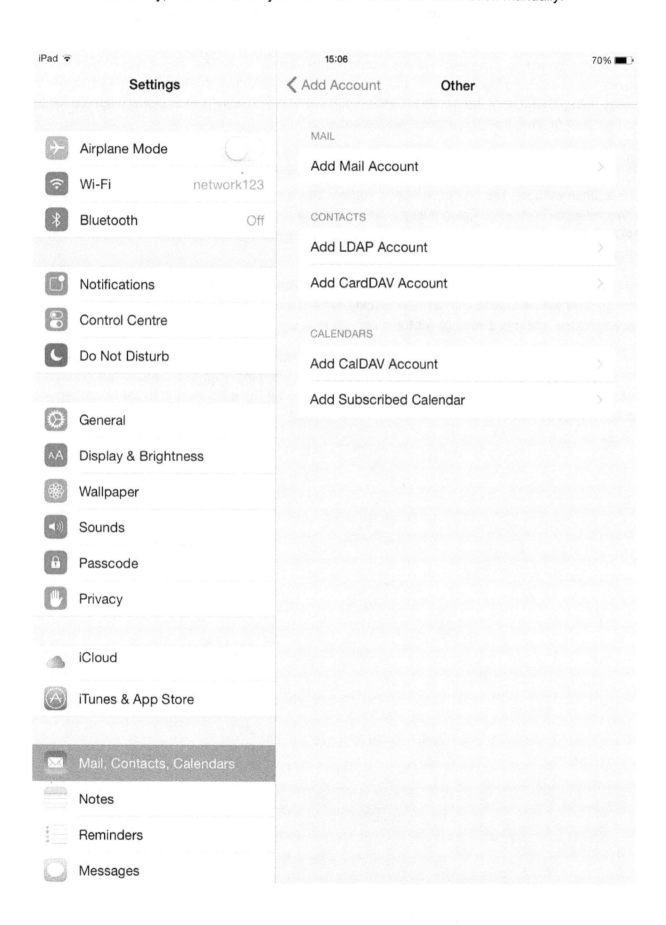

Find out from your email provider if your account uses IMAP or POP, and tap on the relevant type. Then, enter the host name, username, and password for your incoming server, the host name for your outgoing server and, if it is required, the username and password for the outgoing server. When you have done this, tap Next.

You will then be asked what services you would like to turn on. Your iPad allows you to sync notes between devices using Mail accounts, but if you would not like to use this service, or if you are already using iCloud, turn the switch off. When you tap save, an activity indicator will appear for a short amount of time, then the account will be added.

If you need to configure more advanced options, such as setting a port for the outgoing mail server, adding extra SMTP servers, or configuring mailbox behaviours, tap on the account name. This will open a small window. Tap on Account, and you will be able to alter the account and incoming mail server settings. To alter outgoing mail server settings, or to add an extra SMTP server, tap on SMTP. From here you will see your primary server, which you can tap on to edit settings, and an option to add extra servers.

If you go back, then tap on advanced, you will be able to change mailbox behaviours and other settings. You will be able to change how quickly deleted messages are permanently removed as well as change advanced settings for the incoming mail server.

Now, if you open the Mail app, you will see that your account and all its emails have been added. If you open the Settings app again, you can configure how often the iPad checks for email. Tap on "Fetch New Data". From here, you have the option to turn off Push email, and to set how often your iPad should check for emails.

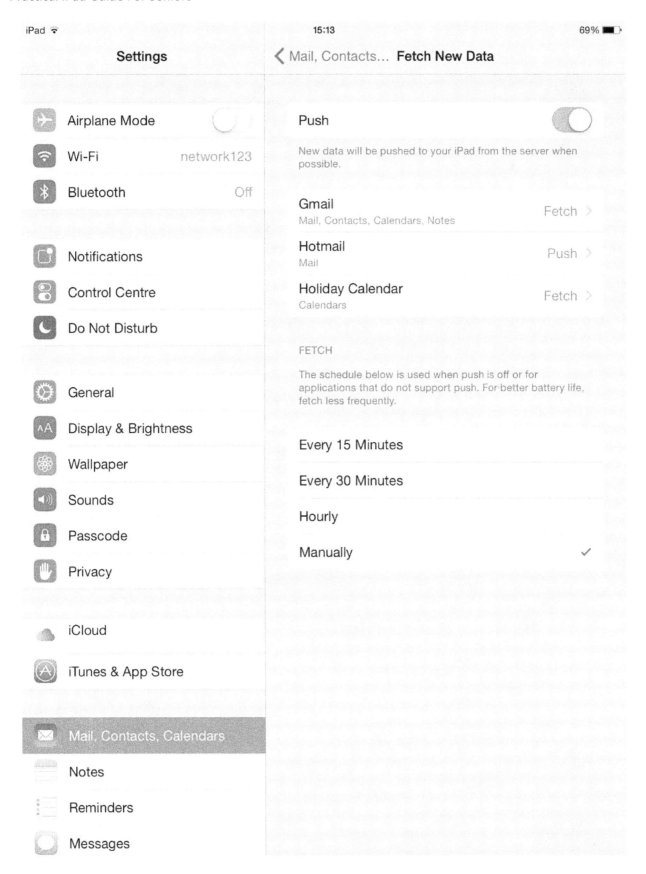

The less frequently your iPad checks, the better your battery life will be. If you set it to "Manually", your iPad won't check for emails until you open the Mail app. This means you won't receive emails as quickly, but could save you a lot of battery life.

Reading, Replying, Forwarding Emails:

In my opinion checking email on an iPad is a more pleasure experience, than reading emails on a computer. You can sit back comfortably and take your time. It's also very easy to do. When you look at your homescreen, the icon for the Mail app will have a badge containing a number. This number indicates how many unread emails you have since you last opened.

Open the Mail app to begin reading.

The last email you read should automatically appear on screen. To read different emails, you can either use the arrow buttons to move through emails, or, if you are in portrait mode tap on the Inbox button to see a full list of all your emails. A shortcut to open this panel is to swipe to the right anywhere in the mail app.

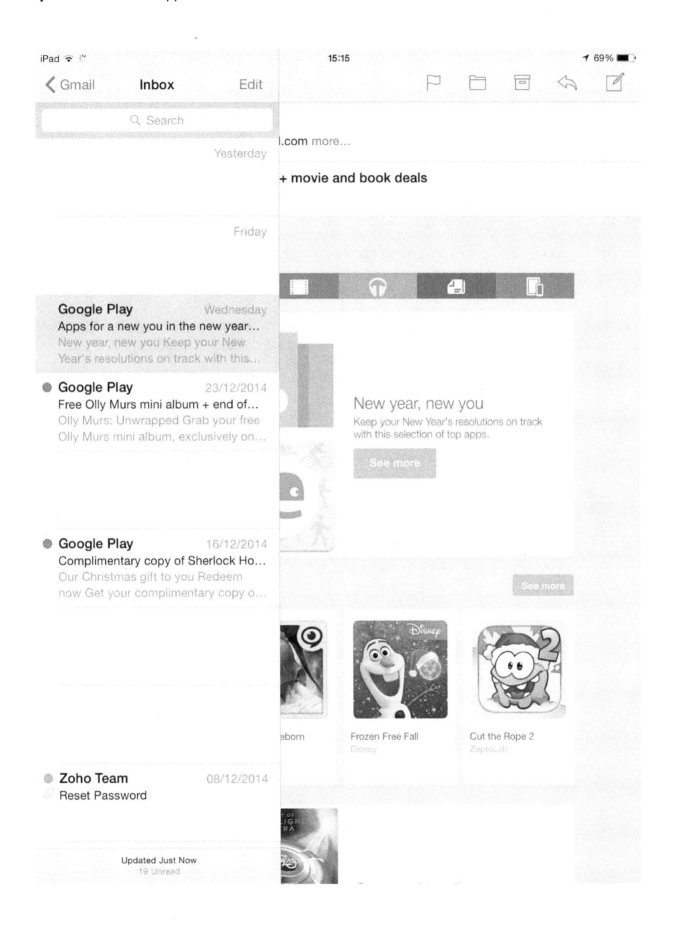

If you are in landscape mode, the list of your emails will always show up on the side. Emails that are unread will have a Blue circle next to them, and emails you have replied to will have an arrow next to them. If an email contains attachments, it will have a paperclip icon next to the sender's name. To open and read your email, you simply need to press on the email you want to open. If you then want to delete it, you can press on the junk symbol on the top header. You can also delete emails that haven't been read from the list view, without opening them. You do this by going into edit mode. Edit mode allows you to perform a number of actions on a list of emails without having to open them first.

A quick word about contacts: The header will show you the contact your email is from. If the person who sent you the email is not already a contact, it's easy to add the person to your contact list. When you do this you'll be given the opportunity to provide some contact information about them, which will be stored on that individual's contact card. You can hide the header information if you wish, by pressing the hide button. This is useful if the email has been sent to a long list of contacts.

To check for new emails, simply drag down on this window and you will see a refresh icon appear. Continue dragging until it turns into an activity indicator. This means your iPad is checking for emails.

If you have multiple accounts, a back button should appear in the top left. Tap on this, and you will see a full list of your accounts and mailboxes. The All Inboxes mailbox is an aggregate of the inboxes for all your mail accounts.

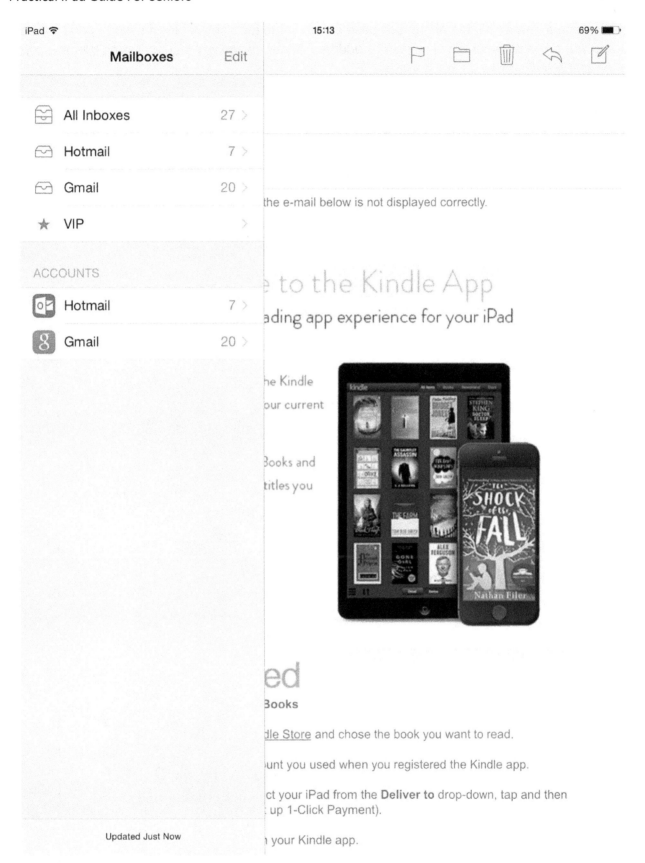

iPad 📶   15:13   69% 🔋

Mailboxes   Edit   🚩   📁   🗑   ↩   ✏️

📨   All Inboxes   27 >

📨   Hotmail   7 >

📨   Gmail   20 >

⭐   VIP   >

ACCOUNTS

📧   Hotmail   7 >

🅖   Gmail   20 >

the e-mail below is not displayed correctly.

e to the Kindle App

ading app experience for your iPad

he Kindle
our current

Books and
titles you

ed

Books

dle Store and chose the book you want to read.

unt you used when you registered the Kindle app.

ct your iPad from the **Deliver to** drop-down, tap and then
up 1-Click Payment).

Updated Just Now   your Kindle app.

To find a particular email, you can use the app search bar to look through all your emails in all your accounts and mailboxes. For more effective searching, you can further narrow your search by adding a relevant word into the search bar. For instance, if you know the email you're looking for was sent on a certain date add this to your search words and receive more relevant results.

To compose a new email, tap on the compose button in the top right. A new message pane will pop up and you can enter your email recipient's address, either by typing it in, or pressing the blue plus button and selecting one of your contacts.

If you tap on "Cc/Bcc", you can select email addresses to send Carbon Copies or Blind Carbon Copies to. In the first instance all the recipients can see who has been included on the email, in the second, they can't. If you have multiple email accounts, you will also be able to select from which one you would like to send the email.

You can then enter a subject and content for the email. You can double tap to select text, then format it to make it Bold, Italics, or Underlined. When you are done, you can tap send, or, if you would like to send the email at a later date, you can tap on Cancel, then save the email as a draft. This action will close the new email screen and you will find yourself back at your inbox. When an email is sent, it will be sent from the account into which it was received, unless instructed otherwise.

To quickly access your draft messages, press and hold on the compose window. A pop-up will appear, with a list of all your drafts. Simply tap on a draft to continue composing it.

If you want to reply to an email, tap on the arrow to the left of the compose button, and tap on Reply.

A compose window will appear, which will quote the old message, and give you a space to write yours at the top.

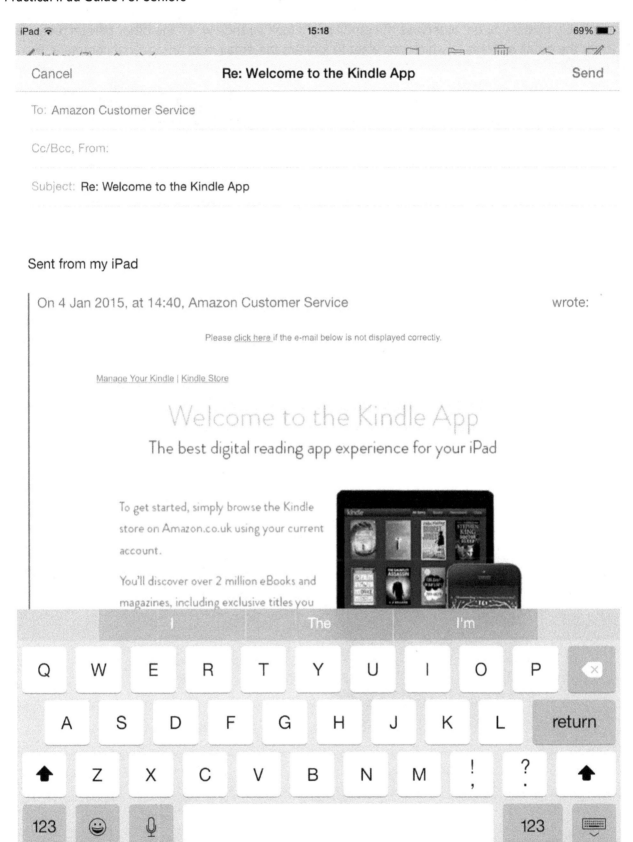

Enter your message, then tap send. Be aware that you will be given the option to reply to either all of the recipients of an email, or just a single one. If you press reply all, it will be sent to everybody originally included in the email.

If you have an interesting message which you want to forward to someone, tap on the arrow again, then press forward. If the message has attachments, you will be asked if you want to include them;

it's probably best if you do, otherwise the email might look strange when the other person receives it. Enter the email address to which you want to forward the email, add an optional comment, then press send.

To change the default email account from which emails are sent, navigate to the Settings app, tap on Mail, Contacts, Calendars, then on Default Account. Once you have selected an account, new messages will be sent from this account by default.

Sending Photos, Attachments, and Links

Email is a very useful tool for sharing things with people. iOS makes it incredibly easy for you to quickly share photos or videos with people through email. First, compose a new message. In the body of the message, press and hold your finger down until the magnifying glass appears, then release. You will see a popup appear with a few options.

Tap "Insert Photo or Video" and you will be presented with a popup with all your photos on.

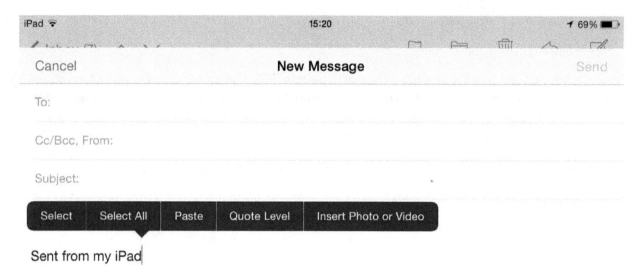

Select on the one you would like to use, and tap use.

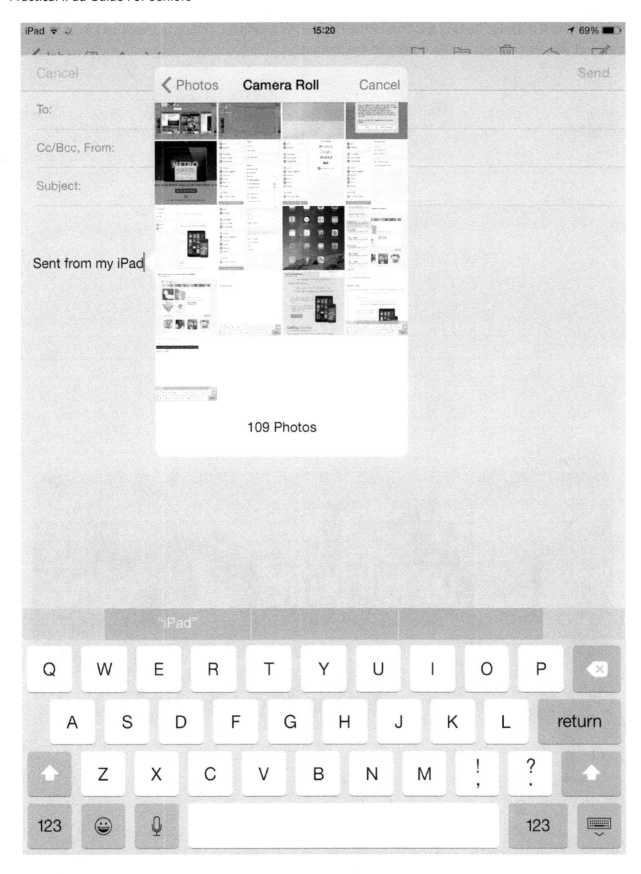

You can repeat this with multiple images, but you need to be careful not to go over the 20mb limit. When you insert a photo, a counter will appear at the top, letting you know how large the email is. Tap on this, and you will be given options for sizing. Setting the size of the images to a smaller setting will reduce the size of an email, but will also impact on the quality of the images.

Only use the actual size of the image if you are sending them to be printed off or manipulated. If you are just sending them to someone so that they can look at the pictures, Large or Medium should be fine. Tap send when you are done, and the email will be sent to the recipient. You can see a progress bar at the bottom of the inbox pane to let you know how much of the message has been sent.

You can also send photos by opening the photos app, tapping edit, selecting the photos you want (a maximum of five per email), then tapping the share button in the top left and selecting Mail.

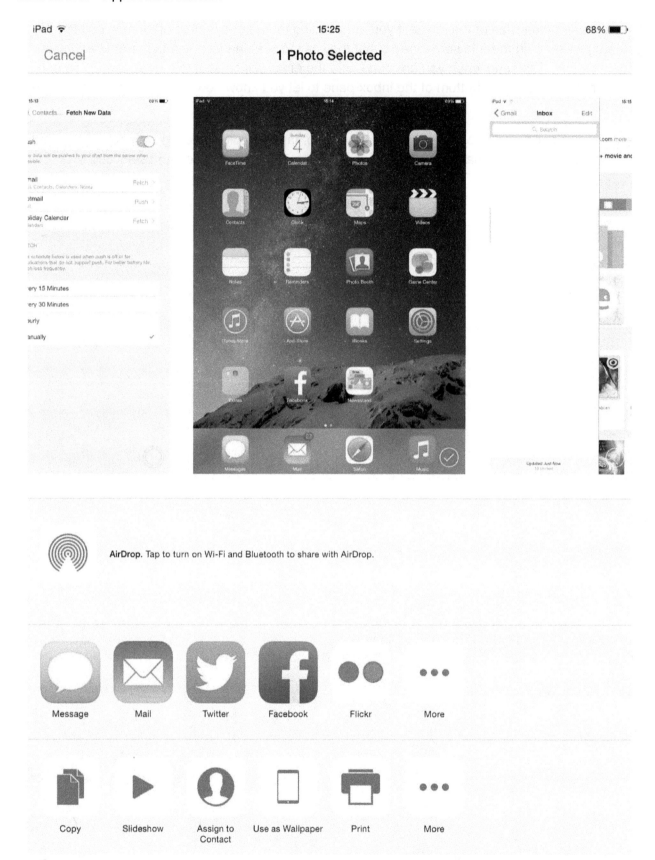

AirDrop. Tap to turn on Wi-Fi and Bluetooth to share with AirDrop.

| Message | Mail | Twitter | Facebook | Flickr | More |

| Copy | Slideshow | Assign to Contact | Use as Wallpaper | Print | More |

In addition to this, you can send individual images by opening them, tapping on the share button in the top right, and selecting mail.

Some apps will also allow you to send content as attachments in emails. For example, Contacts will allow you to Share a contact, and iBooks allows you to email PDFs with people. Many apps from the app store will include this functionality, but the method of sending them may vary.

You can use Safari to send links to people via email. To just send one link, tap the share button, then tap email. If you want to send multiple links in one email, you can use the share button, and tap copy.

Then, switch to the Mail app, and compose a new message. Press and hold so the magnifying glass appears, then tap paste. You can repeat this process for multiple links.

Organising messages

If you receive a lot of messages, keeping your email inbox uncluttered can be difficult. Mail has a few features that can assist you in this task. The most basic is deleting messages. If you have already responded to an email, or if it is no longer of use to you, simply tap on the trash can in the toolbar, and the email will be removed from your inbox. One such feature is VIPs. You can set certain contacts as VIPs, and have an inbox especially for them, so you will only have to see emails from the most important people.

To add a VIP, go to Mailboxes, tap on VIP, then tap Add VIP. You can now select a contact from your address book. If you receive an email from

someone who isn't in your address book, but whom you would still like to be a VIP, you can add them by opening the email, tapping on their name, then tapping on Add to VIP.

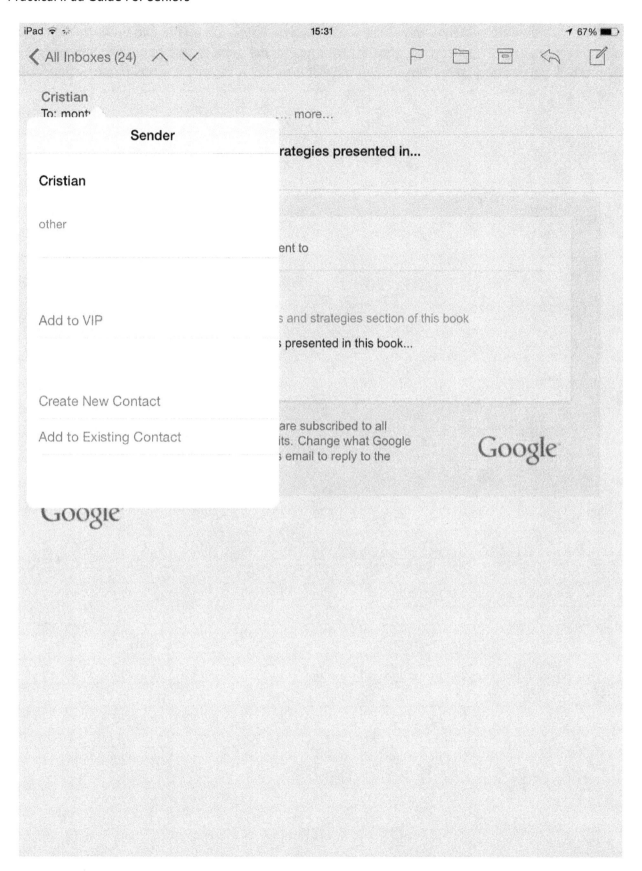

Two more useful features are flagging and marking as unread. To mark a message as unread, tap on the flag in the toolbar, then on Mark as Unread. The email will now have a blue circle next to it, and your unread email count will go up.

If an email is important, you may want to flag it. To flag an email, tap on the flag button in the toolbar, then tap flag. A flag icon will appear to the right of the subject, and to the left of the email in your inbox. If you go back to mailboxes, you will also see that a flagged mailbox has now appeared, containing all the messages you have flagged.

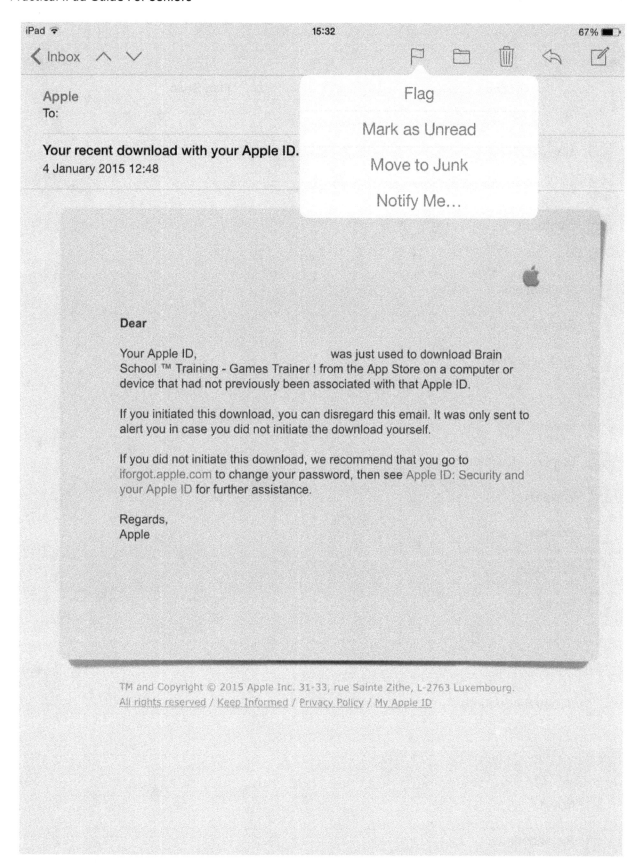

If you don't like the orange default flag, you can change it to an orange dot instead. The dot is like the new message alert (but it's orange, not blue). To change the flagging symbol, press settings on the home screen, then press on "Mail, Contacts and Calendars". You will see the option "Flag style" and be able to make your choice of flag or dot here!

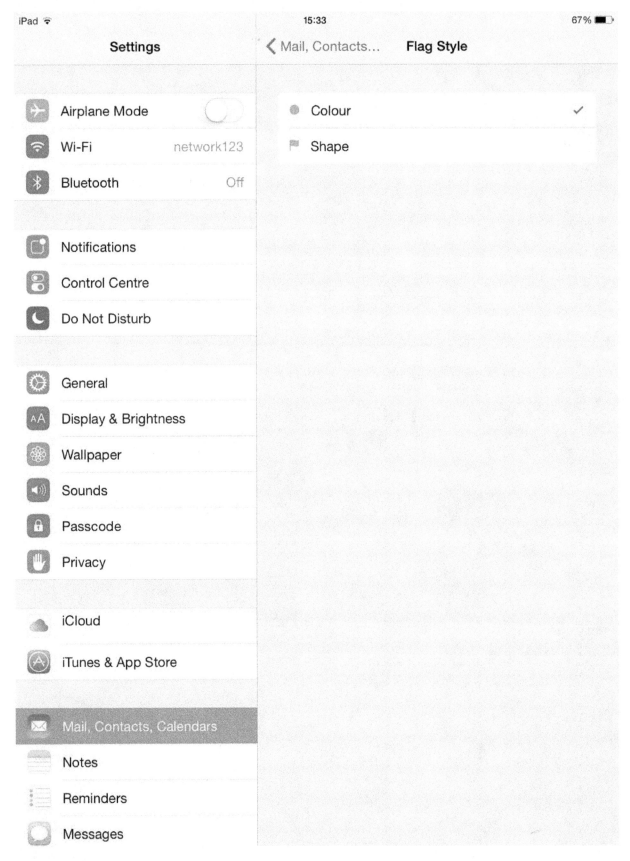

A final feature Mail offers to help you keep organised is mailboxes. When you only have one email account set up, you'll need to press the new mailbox button to do this. If you have various email accounts, you'll need to go into the account setting again before you can create a new mailbox for it. Your mailboxes are located on the left hand side. Mailboxes are the folders which house your emails. You will have at least one mailbox per email account, but you are able to create many more, to help you get organised. They're useful for keeping receipts or other documents together in one place.

To create a new mailbox in an email account, go back to Mailboxes, and tap on the account in which you would like to create a new mailbox. Tap edit in the top corner, then new mailbox in the bottom. Enter a name, and ensure that the mailbox location is correct, then press save. It may take a few seconds, but an email inbox will now be created.

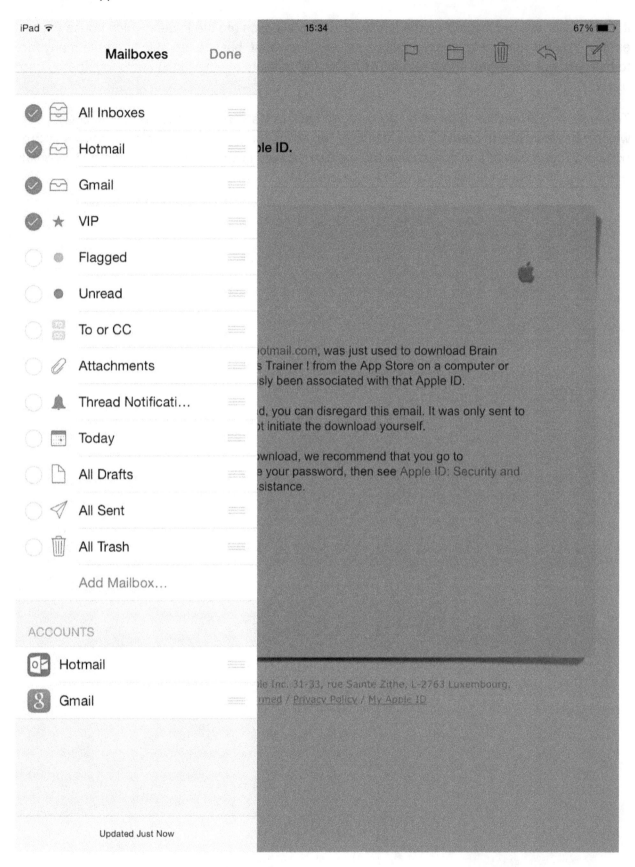

To put an email in an inbox, tap on the folder icon in the toolbar, then select the folder to which you would like to move it. The email will then be moved into the folder.

Setting up signatures for Mails

The default signature in Mail is "Sent from my iPad". You can change this by opening the Settings app, going to the Mail, Contacts, Calendars pane, then tapping on Signature. In the text box you can enter a signature which will be put at the foot of all your emails by default. You can even add bold, underlined, or italic text. If you wish to have different signatures for different accounts, you can select "Per Account". You will then be presented with multiple text boxes in which to edit your signature for each email account.

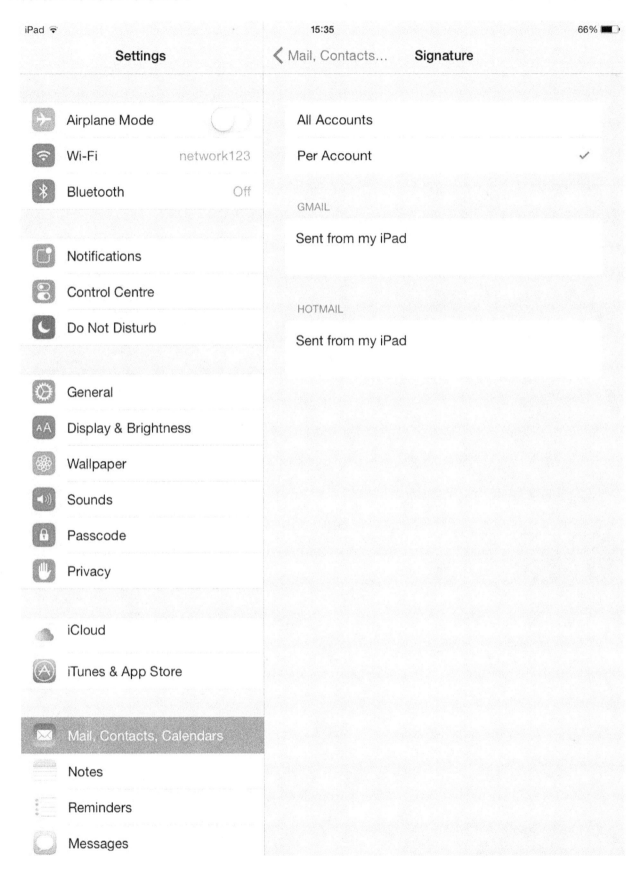

Now, when you tap compose, you will see your new signatures appear in the bottom of emails.

iCloud mail

Setting up iCloud mail will ensure that you can get hold of your mail (and mailboxes) from any Apple device.To set up your iCloud account, go into settings on your homescreen and then press "iCloud". Sign in with your Apple ID or iCloud.com email address and then tap it to turn on Mail

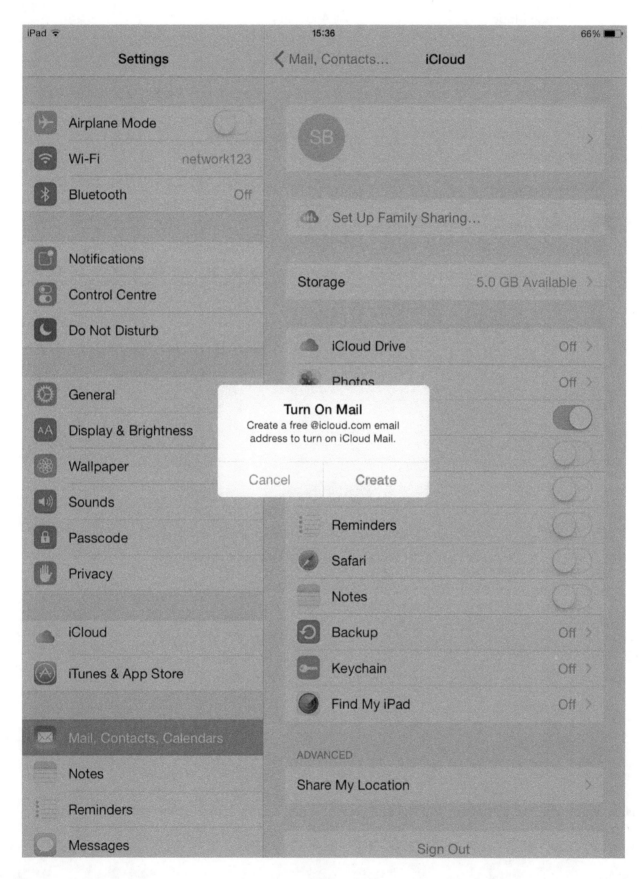

Finally there's a shortcut you can use to erase text in the Mail app of your iPad. You shake it! It even works when you need to redo text that you've erased by accident! As well as getting rid of text, you can use shake to undo if you've just archived, filed or deleted emails incorrectly.When you use shake to undo, shake your device lightly. A prompt will appear and allow to delete your previous action.

Browsing Web & Working with Safari

Connecting to WiFi

WiFi allows you to connect to the internet without having to use mobile data, and is often quicker. On iPads without 3G, it is the only method of getting online. To connect to a new WiFi network, open the Settings app and tap on WiFi. Make sure the switch is turned on, then wait for the iPad to discover some networks.

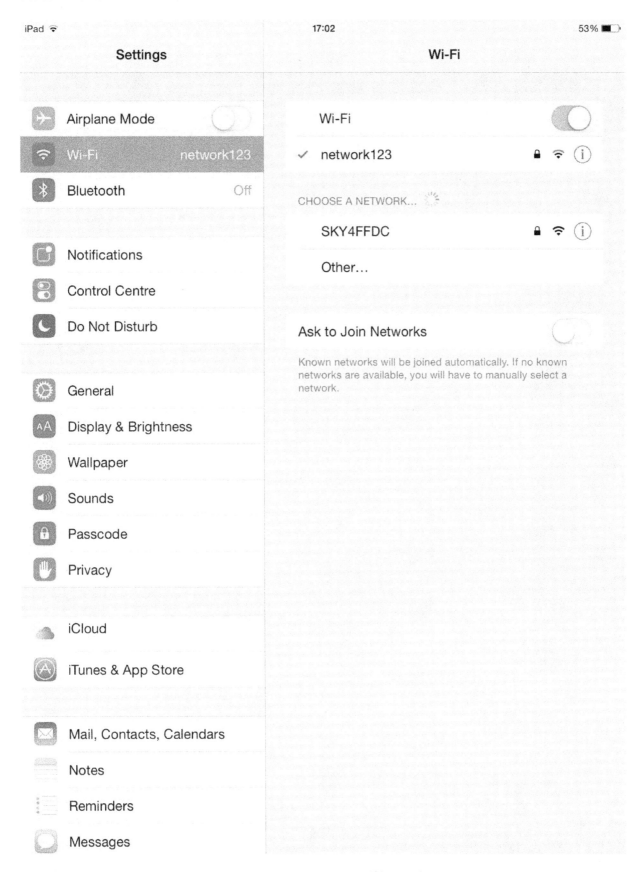

When the one you want to connect to appears, tap on it. If it requires a password, you will be asked to enter it. This is indicated by the padlock icon.

A blue tick will appear next to the network name when it is connected. If you want to connect to a network that is hidden, tap on "Other". You will then be asked to enter the network name and configure the security settings. These will vary between networks.

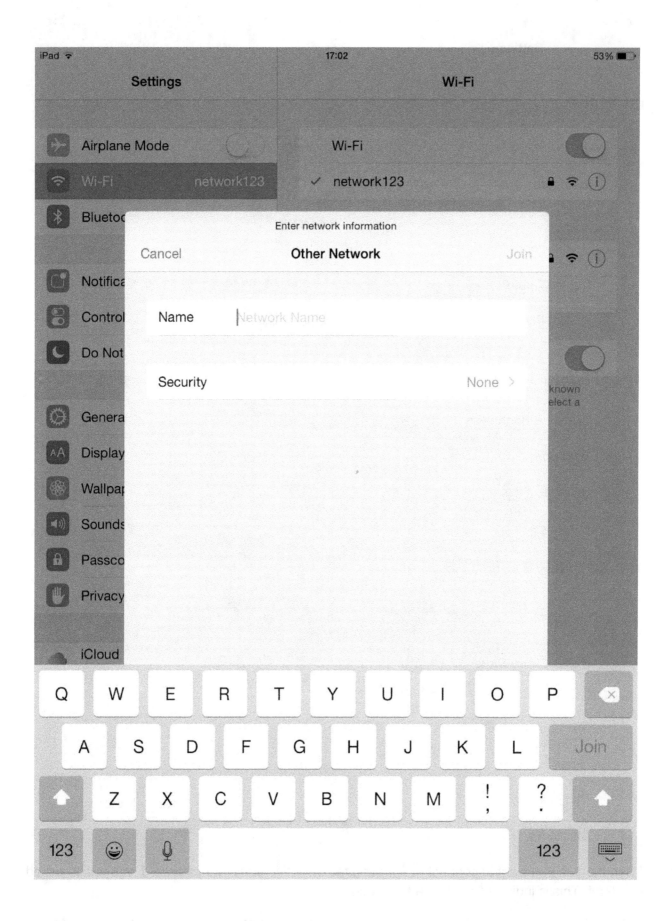

Once you are connected to any network, your iPad will automatically reconnect to it when it becomes available. If you do not want this to happen, tap on the blue arrow next to the network name, then tap "Forget this Network", and the alert that follows it.

If you want to find a WiFi hotspot, the fastest way to find them is to ask Siri "Where are WiFi hotspots?" or you could ask for hotspot information for a geographical area. For example you could ask "Where are WiFi hotspots in London?"

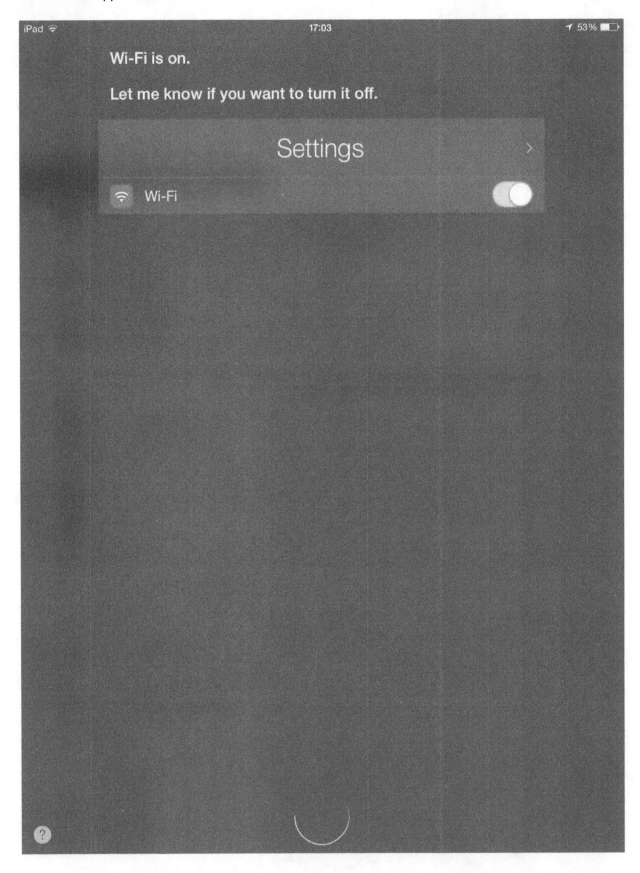

A final option available in the WiFi settings is "Ask to Join Networks". If you have this turned on, you will be asked if you want to connect to a network when none of your known networks are available, but there are other ones that you could connect to. In some cases this can be useful, but the alert can often be disruptive if you keep walking past networks.

If you're having trouble connecting to available WiFi networks, you can try rebooting your iPad. Hold down the Home and Power buttons to do this. If this doesn't work, you could try rebooting your networks. For this you'll need to go into Settings, then General, then Reset, then Reset Network Settings.

Using Mobile Data

WiFi is normally the fastest, and cheapest way to connect to the internet, but when a WiFi network is unavailable, mobile data can be very useful. Mobile Data is only available on iPads with 3G/4G and WiFi, not WiFi only models. These iPads will have black plastic on their backs, and a slot for a SIM card.

Firstly, you will need to insert a Micro SIM card. You can purchase iPad SIMs from many different providers, either on pay as you go or monthly plans. To insert the SIM, find a flat surface that will not scratch the iPad's screen, or use the Smart Cover as protection, and place it face down.

Then, find the small silver tool that came with the iPad, or a paperclip. Insert the tool into the hole next to the SIM slot at a 45-degree angle and push. The sim tray should eject slightly. Remove the SIM tray, then place the Micro SIM it, being careful not to touch the gold contacts. You will only be able to place it in one way, due to the shape of the card. Then insert the tray back into the iPad, with the SIM card facing downwards. It should click into place.

Now, unlock your iPad, open up the Settings app, and tap on Mobile Data. To use Mobile Data, turn the switch on. In the top left, you will see your iPad searching for connectivity. When it finds the network, your carrier's name should appear, along with an icon illustrating that the iPad is connected to either 4G, 3G, Edge, or GPRS.

In the Mobile Data settings, you can choose to turn Data Roaming on or off. If you have it on, your iPad will use data when you are abroad, which can result in extra costs. You shouldn't have to change the APN Settings, unless your iPad won't connect to Mobile Data, in which case you should call your carrier.

You will also be able to set options for what should be able to use Mobile Data. The fewer things you turn on, the less data your iPad will use, so only turn on the things you really need.

It is possible to see which apps are using the most mobile data by going into settings and viewing the third-party app information listed here. This will give you an idea of how much data each app uses, although the results are not live. They will show you how much data the app has used on your iPad historically. You can use this information to make a decision about removing non-essential apps that are draining your data.

Below this you can see applications for your SIM, which will vary between carriers, and an option to set a SIM PIN, which can prevent people using your SIM card if it is stolen, or when your iPad is restarted.

Using the Safari Browser

The default application for browsing in your iPad is Safari:

However, your iPad will give you a few browsing options.

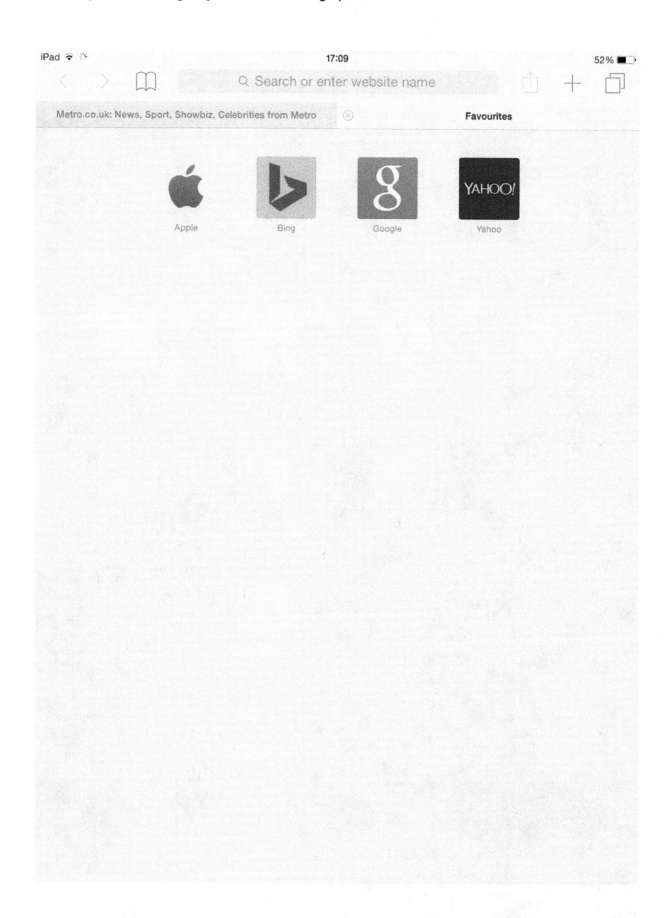

When you open Safari, you will see a bar at the top with some buttons and two text boxes, a tab bar, and an area where web pages will load. The webpages you use most frequently will helpfully pre-load in this area, before you begin any new searches.

iPad 🛜   17:13   51% 🔋

<   >   📖   metro.co.uk   ↻   ⬆   +   ⧉

Ⓧ Metro.co.uk: News, Sport, Showbiz, Celebrities from Metro   Favourites

NEWS... BUT NOT AS YOU KNOW IT

34.6M SHARES

| HOME | NEWS | SPORT | ENTERTAINMENT | LIFESTYLE | MORE ⌄ | 🔍 |

This is the clearest photo of 'Bigfoot' ever taken

Oh Photoshop, this there anything you can't do? »

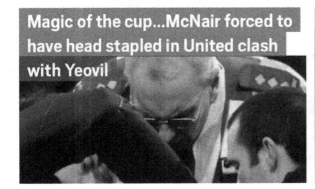

Magic of the cup...McNair forced to have head stapled in United clash with Yeovil

Nine year journey to reach Pluto for first time

The first text box is the address field. In here you can enter the address of a website in order to be taken to it. To the right of that, there is a search field. In here you can enter search terms. When you tap in the text box, a popup will appear, showing your recent searches. When you start typing, suggestions for what you might be searching for will appear. To search for something, either tap on a suggestion, or tap "search" on the keyboard.

To navigate web pages, you can scroll horizontally or vertically, pinch to zoom in and out, tap on links, and double tap on areas of the page you would like to focus on, such as articles and images. Two fingered swipes will scroll between Safari tabs and this two fingered pinch outwards will display the centred Safari tab. A two fingered pinch inwards will display the tabs with live content, when you have more than one tab open.

To go back a page, tap on the back arrow in the top left. To go forward, tap on the forward arrow. If you want to refresh the page you are currently on, tap on the Refresh button in the right hand side of the address bar.

If you are reading an article, the Safari Reader can improve the experience. When Safari detects that you are reading an article, a button will appear in the address bar. Tap on it, and the Reader will appear. The page will now be formatted in a way that should be easier to read. You can increase and reduce font size by tapping on the two A's in the top left, then tapping on the buttons that appear.

If you're finding adverts distracting, you can enable reader mode, which will turn the website you're reading into text, photos and videos, without any of the attention-grabbing ads. To do this open the webpage you want to read and then press this small button here with the lines on.

metro.co.uk

A A

This is the clearest photo of 'Bigfoot' ever taken

Bigfoot, possibly (Picture: John Rodriguez)

We might have managed to land a probe on a comet in 2014, but that doesn't necessarily mean the human race has grown any smarter over the past year.

Indeed, 2015 has kicked off with a slightly less scientific breakthrough – someone claims they have taken the clearest ever photo of Bigfoot.

John Rodriguez, a 66-year-old retired electrician, sent the totally legitimate picture to the Huffington Post, claiming he photographed the mythical beast while fishing in Florida on boxing day.

You can also print or email the content of Safari Reader, for example a particular website, by tapping on the share sheet to the left of the address bar, and selecting an icon.

If you have iCloud enabled, you can use iCloud tabs. This allows you to sync open tabs between iOS and Mac devices. For example, if you were viewing an interesting website on your Mac and wanted to look at it on your iPad, you just have to tap on the Cloud icon in Safari, then tap on the website. There are more options available for Safari. Open the Settings app and tap on Safari. From here you can: set the default Search Engine to Google, Yahoo!, or Bing; tell Safari to open new tabs in the background; set the bookmarks bar to always be shown; enable private browsing, which allows you to look at websites without your history being logged; change preferences for accepting cookies; clear your web history; delete the cookies data sites may have stored on your device; disable JavaScript; and set options for blocking popup windows.

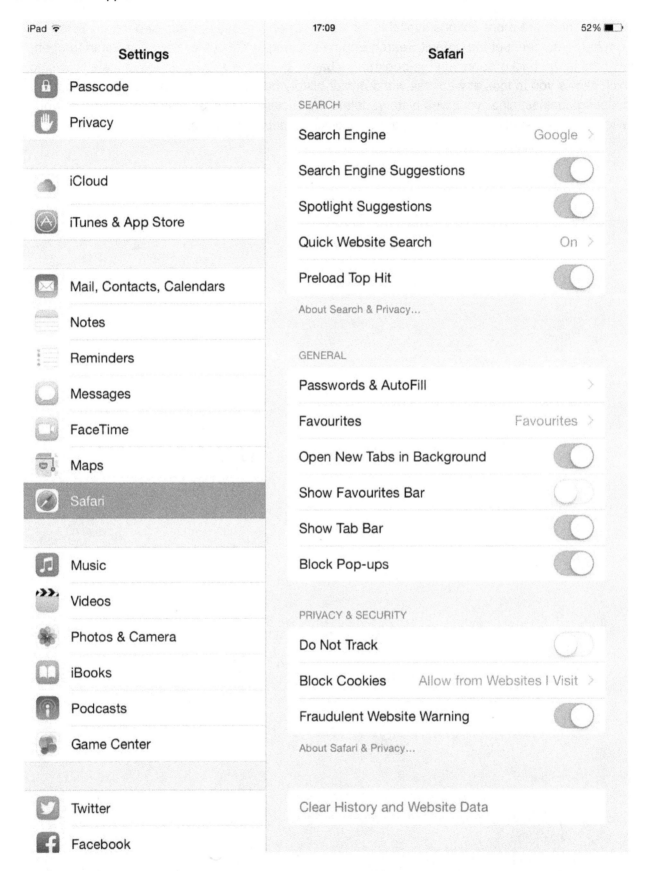

Another useful setting is AutoFill. This means that Safari can use your contact information to automatically complete forms on the Internet. To set it up, turn AutoFill on, then tap on your contact card. You can also set AutoFill to remember your usernames and passwords for websites. To use

AutoFill, navigate to a website with a form, tap in the first field, and then press the AutoFill button that appears on the keyboard. Make sure you check the form in case there are any errors.

In the Settings, you can turn fraud warning on and off. Fraud Warning will tell you when a site is possibly fraudulent. Such sites may try to mimic others in order to obtain some of your personal information, or payment details. Of course, it may not catch every fraudulent site, so you still need to be careful.

Finally, by going to Advanced, and Website Data, you can see how much data websites have stored on your iPad, and delete the data for individual websites that you don't plan on using again.

Privacy and Security

It's very simply to enter private browsing mode. You simply need to press the "private browsing" button and you will be able to use Safari without being traced. Press this button to leave private browsing.

Cookies remember and record information about you and how you use the internet. To block cookies, you need to go into your settings menu, tap on Safari and then find Privacy & Security. Select "Block cookies". It's up to you to decide between "always" "From third parties and advertisers and "never". You can also enable "Do Not Track" here.

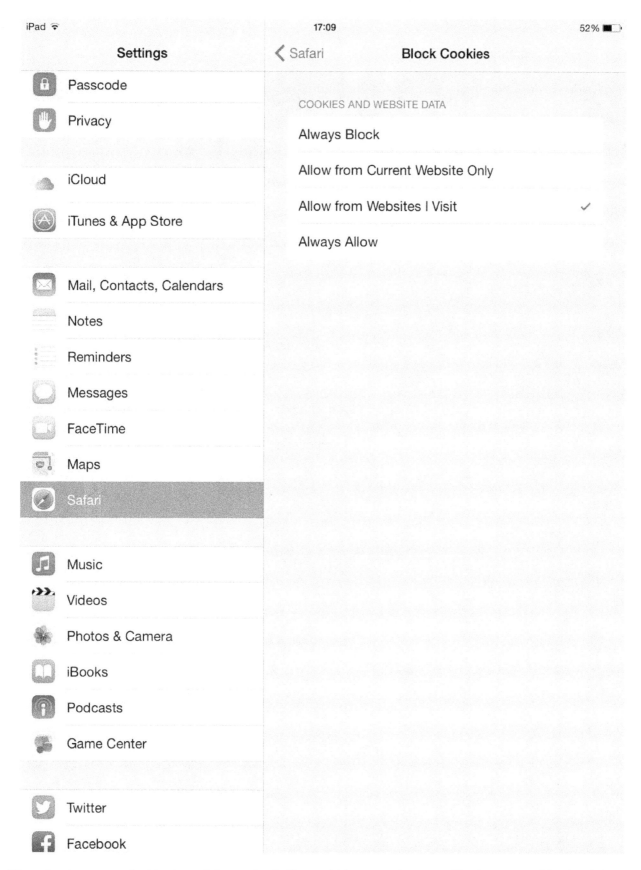

There's also a way to block certain content. If your kids are using your iPad, you can block adult content on it here in Settings. Press "General", then "Enable restrictions" and set up a passcode.

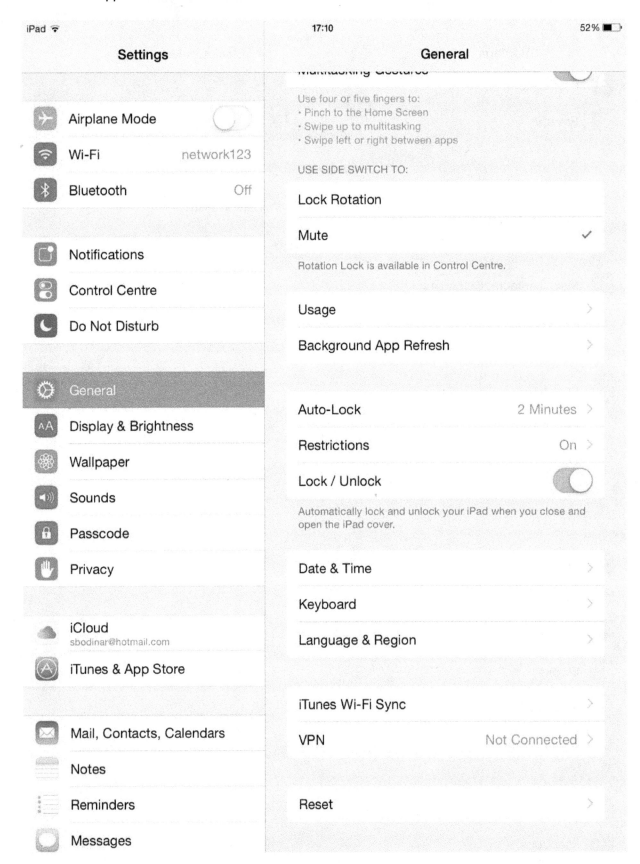

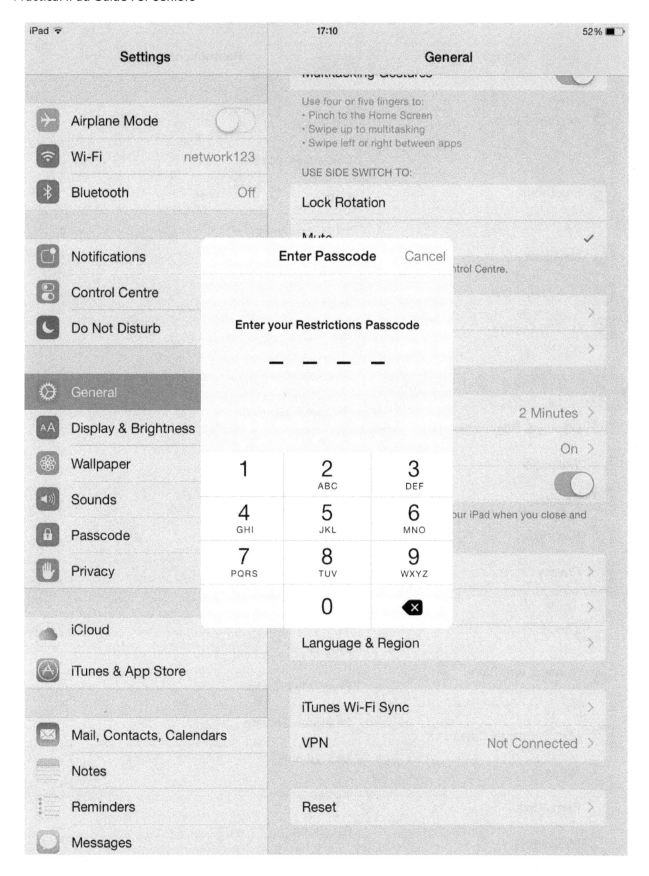

 After this you'll need to tap on "allowed content", then "websites". Next tap "Allowed websites" and finally "Limit adult content."

Mike Jeffries – AppleVideoHub.com

Settings

✈️ Airplane Mode ⬜

📶 Wi-Fi   network123

🔵 Bluetooth   Off

🔔 Notifications

🎛️ Control Centre

🌙 Do Not Disturb

⚙️ General

🔠 Display & Brightness

🌼 Wallpaper

🔊 Sounds

🔒 Passcode

✋ Privacy

☁️ iCloud

Ⓐ iTunes & App Store

✉️ Mail, Contacts, Calendars

📝 Notes

📋 Reminders

💬 Messages

‹ General   Restrictions

ALLOWED CONTENT:

Ratings For   United Kingdom ›

Music & Podcasts   Explicit ›

Films   All ›

TV Programmes   All ›

Books   All ›

Apps   All ›

Siri   All ›

Websites   All ›

Require Password   15 minutes ›

Require password for purchases.

PRIVACY:

Location Services ›

Contacts ›

Calendars ›

Reminders ›

Photos ›

Share My Location ›

Bluetooth Sharing ›

Microphone ›

Twitter ›

Facebook ›

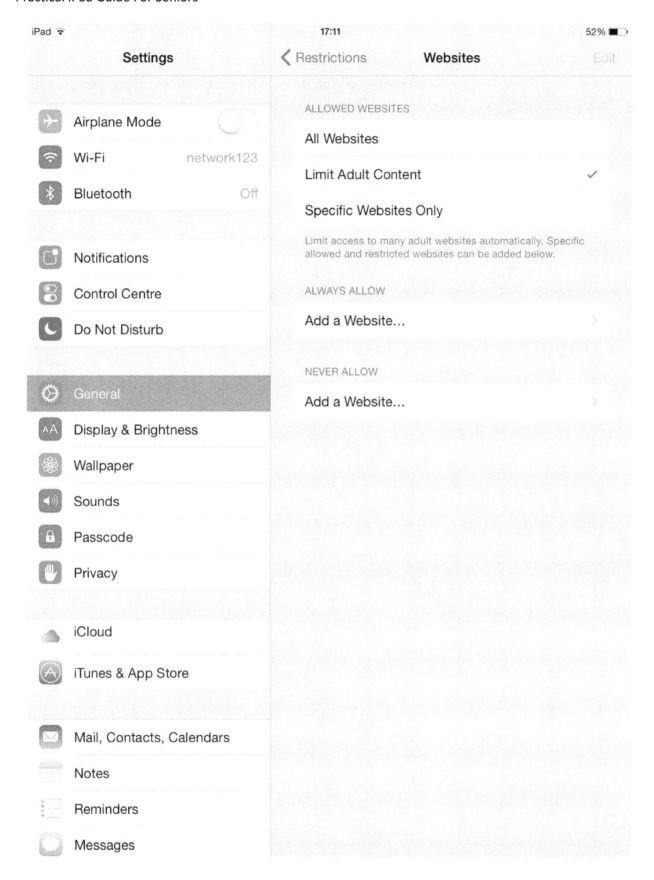

To block a particular website, you'll need to tap here, on "add a website" and then "never allow." You'll need to enter the full website address of the website you'd like to block. If you'd rather control the websites that your children can visit, you'll need to block everything except the websites you allow.

To do this press General in your Settings menu. Tap "Enable Restrictions", set the passcode, then tap "Allowed Content" then "Websites" then "Specific Websites Only." Tap "Done" when you've finished.

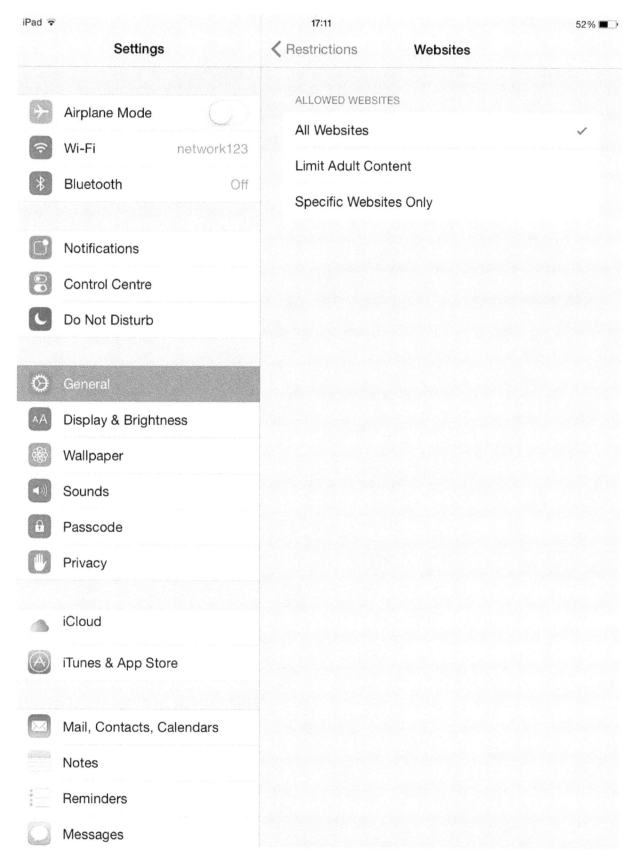

ME

The private browsing button is also useful if you want to close all Safari tabs at once. Press it and you'll be asked if you want to keep all your tabs open or if you want to close them. Press "Close All" and then press the private button again to cancel private browsing.

Bookmarks and Reading List

If you visit a site regularly or want to remember a certain website, you can add it as a bookmark. To do this, tap on the share sheet to the left of the address bar, then tap "Bookmark".

A popup will appear, allowing you to enter a name for the bookmark (which will by default be the page title) and choose where to store it. When you tap on this button, you will be given a list of folders in which you can store the bookmark. Select a folder, then press save. Now, if you tap on the bookmarks button, you will see your new bookmark, along with a number of default bookmarks.

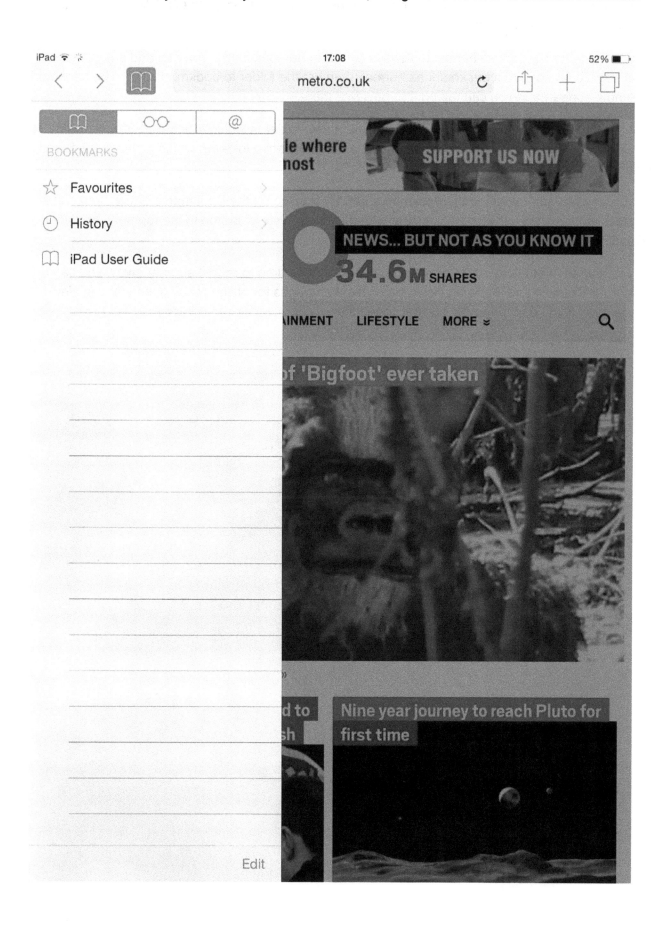

If you decide you want to remove a bookmark, tap the edit button in the top

right of the popover, tap the button to the left of the bookmark, then on the Delete button. You can rearrange the bookmark order by tapping and dragging.

If you have the bookmarks bar set to Always Show, in Safari settings, you can add a bookmark to this bar. To do so, add a bookmark as normal, then set the folder to bookmarks bar. The bookmark will now appear, and you can tap on it to navigate there.

When you are in edit mode, you can also create a new folder in which to store your bookmarks. Tap on the New Folder button in the top left, enter a name, select a folder in which it should be stored, then press Done on the keyboard.

You can even add folders to the bookmarks bar. By tapping on the Bookmarks button, you can also access your History, which you can clear with this "clear history" button in the top right, and your Reading List.

If you find an interesting article or website, but don't have time to read it straight away, you can add it to your Reading List. Reading List even saves web pages for offline reading, so you can view the page even if you don't have an internet connection.

To add a page to the reading list, tap on the share button, and tap "Add to Reading List". You can also press and hold on links, then tap "Add to Reading List" to save them to the Reading List. A loading icon may appear to show that the page is being downloaded.

Now, when you want to read these webpages, simply tap on the bookmarks bar, then on the glasses button at the bottom, and then open any of the web pages in your reading list. It's also possible to view a list of links shared by people you follow on Twitter. Press on the bookmark icon and "shared links"

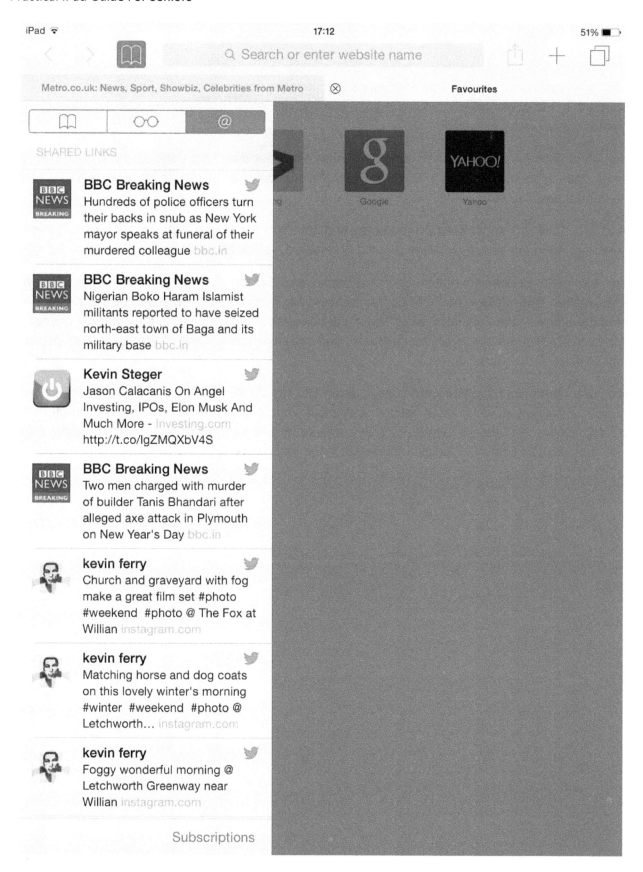

If you have enabled it in iCloud settings, your bookmarks and Reading List will also sync between your iOS and Mac devices.

Bookmarklets

Many browsers allow you to install extensions that improve your experience. The iPad doesn't support this, but bookmarklets provide a good alternative Here's how to install a bookmarklet to download a webpage as a PDF:

First, go to "joliprint.com/ipad, then tap on the share sheet, and add the page as a bookmark. You can set the title to something like "Save as PDF". If you would like quick access, set the folder to the bookmarks bar. Tap save.

Then, tap in the box under Step 2, then press and hold until the Loupe appears. Lift your finger off the screen, then tap select all. When the text is selected, you will be able to copy it.

Next, tap on the bookmarks button, open the Bookmarks Bar folder, then tap on edit. You will now be able to tap on the "Save as PDF" bookmark to edit it. Tap in the box where the URL is, then press the cross on the right hand side. Tap in the box once more, and Paste the contents of your clipboard. Then press "done" on the keyboard, and tap anywhere outside of the bookmarks popup to close it.

Now, when there's a page you want to save as a PDF, tap on the "Save as PDF" bookmarklet, and you will be presented with a list of options. If you just want to save the PDF to iBooks or another app, tap "Download", then "Open In...". This is an example of just one bookmarklet. There are many more that you can search for online, and install in the same way.

Setting up Proxies

Some networks require HTTP proxy settings, to connect to them. You will need to find out from your network administrator what proxy settings your network requires.

To enter a proxy, open the Settings app, then tap on WiFi. When you are connected to the network you would like, tap on the blue arrow. The proxy settings are at the bottom of this screen.

First, tap on either Manual or Auto, depending on the type of proxy your network requires. Then, enter in the relevant details. Your iPad will automatically use these settings when you attempt to connect to the Internet.

Accessibility

Search with Spotlight

Spotlight is the search function on the iPad, and it allows you to search for apps, contacts, emails, notes, reminders, calendar events, and even beyond your device to the internet.

Spotlight is accessible from any homescreen. To use Spotlight, touch the screen away from an app icon or folder and drag your finger down. If you swipe too high near the clock, you might find Notification Centre is displayed. If this happens, try again, swiping from lower. The background will dim, the keyboard will appear and there will be a search box at the top.

In this box, you can type in your search query. For example, if I wanted to search for the Kindle app, I would type "Kindle". If you have folders on your iPad, Spotlight will even tell you what folder the app is in.

Spotlight can also search the content of notes and emails. Simply enter some content you may wish to search for, and anything relevant will appear.

Once a searched-for file appears, you can hover over the file and a preview of the file will appear to ensure you've selected the correct one. When you find the file you're after, you can highlight it and then press ctrl + I and this will provide you with information about the file, such as the file's properties.

Using Spotlight, you can also search the web and Wikipedia. Just type in a search query, then tap "Search Web" or "Search Wikipedia".

To change which order search results appear in, or to prevent certain things from appearing, open the Settings app, tap on General, then on "Spotlight Search".

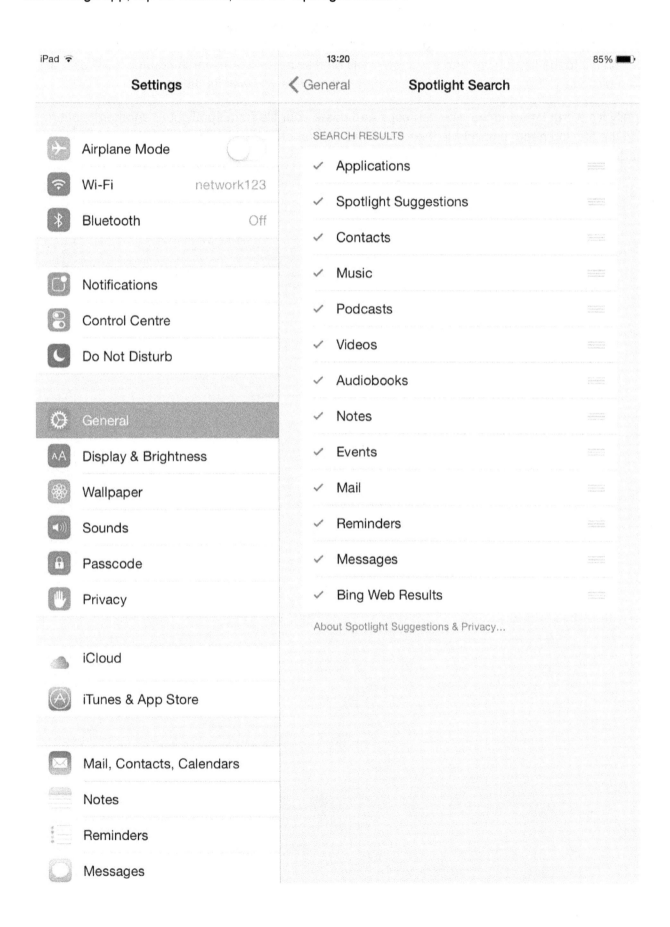

From here you will see a list of content that Spotlight can search for. Tap on an item in the list to activate or deactivate it, or use the three lines on the right to drag it up and down in the list.

Spotlight can often speed up your usage of the iPad, giving you a quick way to access your content from many different parts of the iPad. It can perform calculations for you too, like a calculator. Type your sum into the search bar and the answer will be displayed in the search results. It will also act like a dictionary. Type in a word and the results will provide you with its definition.

Finally it's worth knowing that you can copy and paste your file from spotlight to another location. Find the file you need, highlight it, then press the copy shortcut, which is ctrl + C. Use the paste shortcut ctrl+ V to paste the file into its new location.

Enabling Large Text

If you have impaired vision, or just sometimes find the text on the iPad to be too small, you can enable large text. To do this, open the Settings app, tap on General, then scroll down to Accessibility and tap on it.

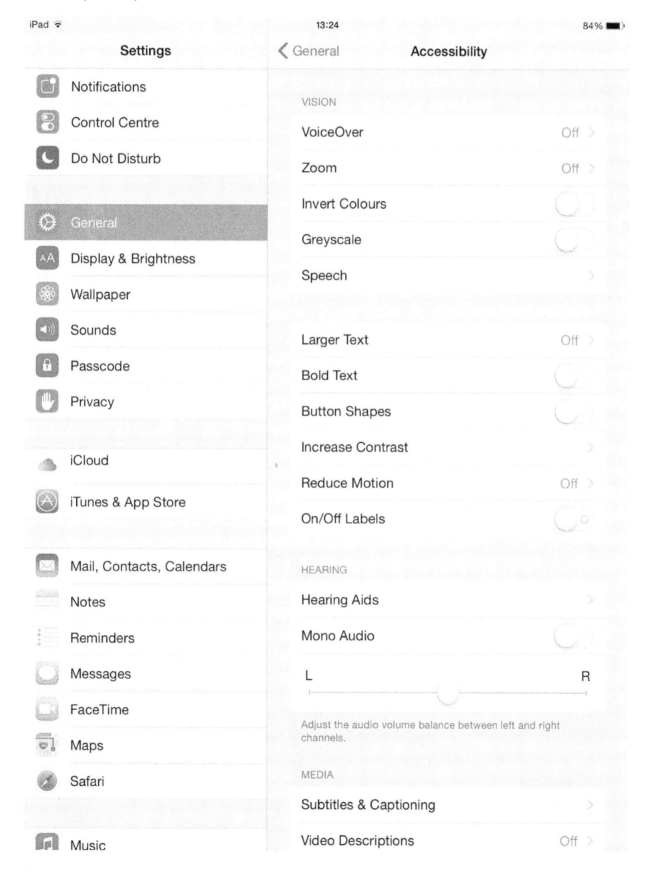

Tap on "Large Text" under the vision section. From here, you can select a text size that is right for you.

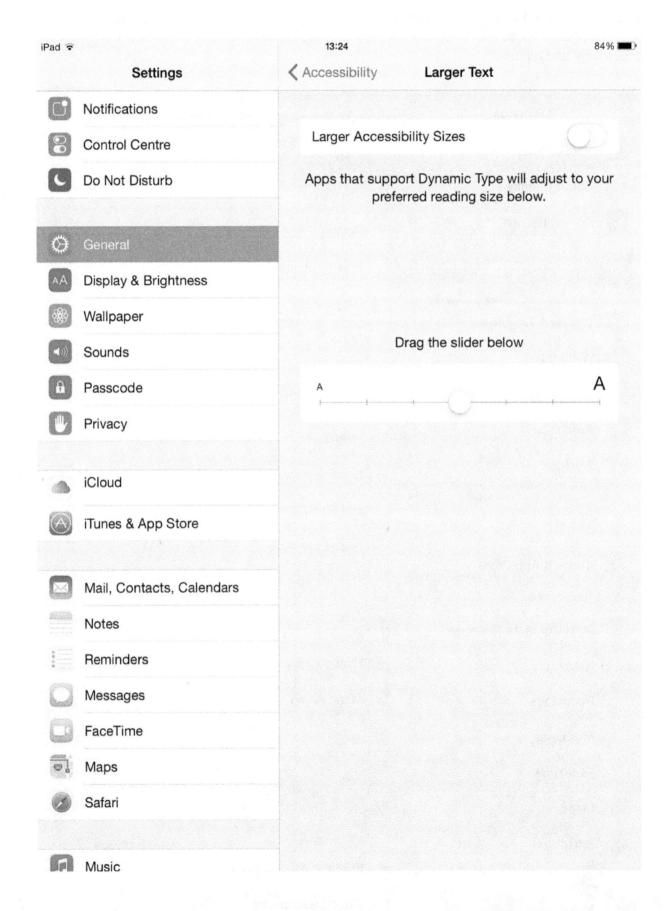

This large text will not display in all apps; only Mail, Contacts, Calendars, Messages, and notes will be affected. Now, when you open one of these

apps, you will see that the text is much larger, and hopefully more readable.

Facebook/Twitter Integration

iOS allows you to integrate your Twitter and Facebook accounts with the operating system. To add an account, open the Settings app, then scroll down in the left pane until you get to Twitter and Facebook. To add a Twitter account, tap on Twitter, enter your username and password, then tap Sign In.

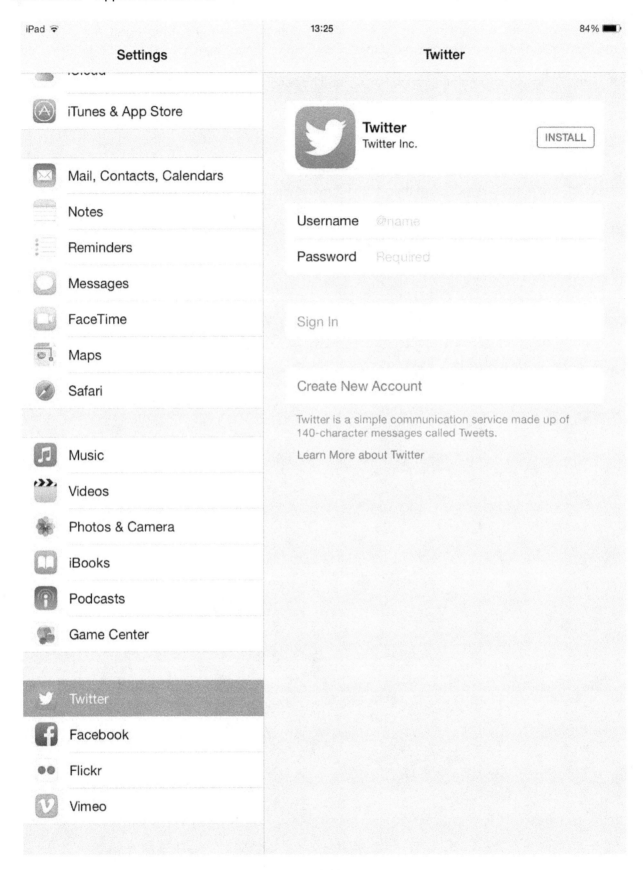

In a few seconds, your account will be added. When you are signed in, you will be asked if you want to install the Twitter app. This is up to you. With Twitter, you can add multiple accounts. To do so, just tap "Add Account" and enter your username and password for that account. You can also add Twitter usernames and pictures to contacts in your address book, whom you follow on Twitter. To do so, tap Update Contacts.

With Facebook, you are limited to adding one account. To do so, tap on Faceboook, enter your email address and password, then tap "Sign in."

A window will appear, telling you what signing into Facebook will allow you to do. Tap "Sign In", in the top right. When you are signed in, you will be asked if you want to install the Facebook app. Again, this is up to you.

Now, all of your Friends' birthdays, and any events you are going to, will appear in your calendar. If you do not want this, turn the Calendar switch off. In addition to this, contacts without pictures in your address book, will have their Facebook photo automatically added. Now you are ready to use the accounts.

Previously there was a useful feature in iOS called the Share Widget and it was located in the Notification Centre. It allowed you to open the Notification Centre, and post a status or tweet without leaving the app you are in. This disappeared in the iOS7 version. However if you install "Share widget for iOS7" it's almost as if the original share widget never went away! Once you've installed it, you'll need to go into Settings, then Notification Centre. Turn the share widget on, because it's off by default. Finally, select the services you want to use ie Twitter or Facebook.

The Photos app also lets you post photos to Twitter and Facebook. Select a photo you would like to share, tap the share sheet in the top right corner,then click one either the twitter or the Facebook icon.

If you select Twitter, you can optionally add a location to the tweet, add text, then press send.

If you instead choose Facebook, you have the option to add a location and enter text – as with Twitter – but you can also select which album you would like the photo to go in, as well as with whom you would like to share the photo.

Finally, certain apps may use your Twitter and Facebook accounts to send statuses, post photos, or even access your timeline. If an app wants to use your account, you simply have to grant it permission, and it will automatically log you in. That's how to use Facebook and Twitter integration on the iPad.

Fun with Photos

Transferring photos to a PC

There are several ways to transfer photos from your iPad to your PC. Probably the easiest way is via windows explorer. To do this, use a cable to connect your iPad to your PC. Launch windows explorer, a shortcut is the windows button +E.

Find the icon for your iPad on the left hand side and double click it. Find the iPad DCIM file, open it and copy the photos you want to transfer onto your computer. Highlight, click and drag them to where you want them to be stored on your PC.

If you'd rather do it via windows 8, the Scanner and Camera Wizard should automatically open after connecting your iPad with your PC. Click on the magnifying glass icon, type computer and press return. Right click on the icon "your Ipad" and then click on "Import pictures and Videos." Next, click "More options" and then "Browse". Here you can choose where you want import photos to. Your "My pictures" folder in the default location. Apple then recommends that you select "Delete files from device after importing" for more space and better handling. Click "Ok" and then "import".

For Windows 7, the process is very similar. The Autoplay window will appear automatically when you connect your devices. You need to click "Import Pictures and Videos using Windows". Next click "Browse" and choose the import location. Then it's "Ok" and "Import"

Transferring photos from a PC

We're going to have a look at transferring photos from a PC via iTunes but most importantly, as a first step, make a backup of your photos on your PC. Once your photos are on your iPad, you'd have to delete them to lose them, but you may lose the photos from your PC if you switch off syncing in the future. Here's how to make a back up: On your PC, click on your iPad drive. Open DCIM here. Copy the photos you want to transfer and paste them onto your desktop for safekeeping.

Here's how to make the transfer. Use a USB cable to connect your iPad to your PC. The next step is to open iTunes and choose your Ipad under "Devices" here. Click on "photos" on the toolbar, then "sync photos", then "apply." Your photos will be synced. If you're shown a warning, you can copy and paste the photos from your back up to a new folder on your iPad.

Transferring photos to a Mac

On a Mac, the easiest way to transfer photos from your iPad is via iPhoto. Open the iPhoto app, and connect your iPad. It should appear in the sidebar. From here you can click on it and either select photos to import, or import all of them.

If you would like the imported photos to go into separate events, you can tick this box. To name the first event, enter the name in this text box. Your Mac will automatically not import any photos that have already been imported before. Once they have imported, you will see that the photos have appeared in their own event, or multiple events, if they were taken over a number of days.

Transferring photos from a Mac

To get photos on your iPad from your Mac, you have to use iTunes. Open the iTunes app, then select your iPad. Click on Photos in the top toolbar, then tick the sync box. You can either sync all your photos – which will use a lot of room – or sync certain albums, events, and even pictures of certain people.

You also have the option of automatically syncing a few of your most recent events, as well as choosing whether or not to transfer videos. When you have selected all the photos you would like to transfer, press "Apply", and they will begin appearing on your iPad. One thing to remember is that photos synced via iTunes cannot be deleted from the iPad until the next time you sync with your computer.

Organizing, editing, and sharing photos

When you get a lot of photos on your iPad it can become a little difficult to find the one you want.

In iPhoto your photos will be split into three sections: Photos, Shared and Albums. Photos will show you your individual pictures, Shared will show you Shared streams with others through iCloud and Albums will show you the different groups of pictures created, for example Camera Roll, Photo Stream, Panoramas, Video and folders that you have made and named yourself.

Here's how to create albums of your photos. Tap on 'Photos' in the toolbar at the top of the Photos app. Then tap edit in the top right, and tap on the photos you would like to group together into an album.

When you have selected them all, tap on 'Add To...', then 'Add to New Album'. Enter a name for the new album, then tap okay. When you have done this, tap on "Albums" in the top toolbar, and you will see that your photos are now grouped together. You can pinch to peek inside an album, or tap on it to fully open it.

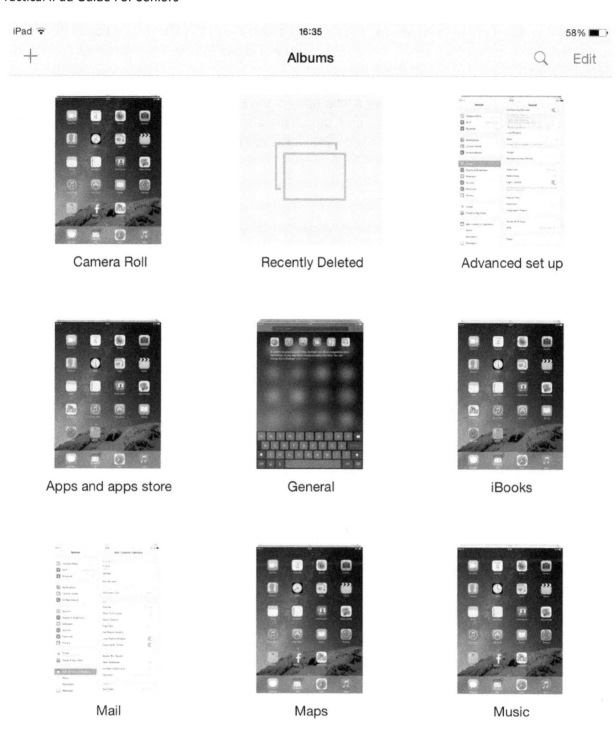

You can repeat this process for all the photos you would like to group together.

If you forget to add a photo to an album, you can add it later.Go to the Photos section of the Photos app, tap edit, then select the image – or images – you would like to add. Then tap 'Add To...', and select the album you would like to move the photos to.

If you have a photo that you feel requires a little editing, the Photos app has a built in function for this. Open a photo you would like to edit, then tap on the edit button. From here you can rotate the image, enhance it automatically, remove red-eyes, and crop it.

When cropping, you can do it manually by pulling in the edges of the image, or by pinching to zoom in. You can also constrain it to various different sizes, if you want to achieve a certain aspect ratio.

If your image is wonky, you can use two fingers to rotate and straighten it. When you are done, press 'Save'.

You can also apply a number of different filters to your image:

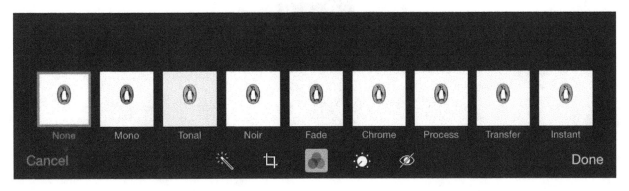

Now that your image is edited, you can share it. To share a single image, open it, click on the action button, then select a share option.

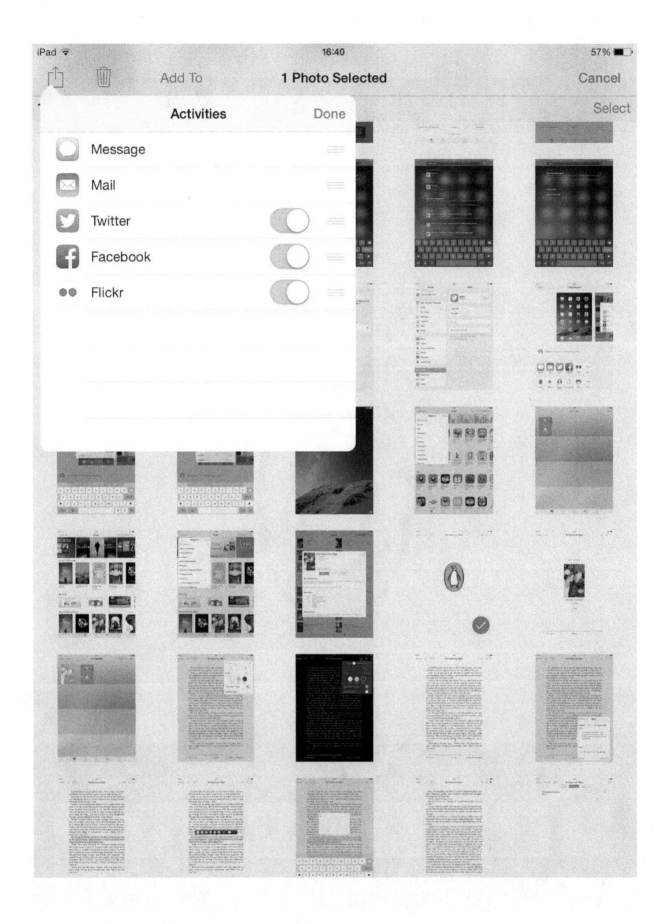

Certain sharing options allow you to send multiple images. Twitter allows only one image at a time, Mail allows you to send up to five images, iMessage allows you to send as many images as you like, so long as they don't exceed 25MB, and you can upload an unlimited amount of photos to Facebook.

In addition to these, you can also use Photo Stream. This allows you to share as many photos as you like with your friends. To share multiple photos to Photo Stream, tap 'Edit', then 'Share', and Select Photo Stream. From here you can enter the names of people you would like to share the photos with, name the photo stream, and decide whether or not to share it publicly.

If you choose to share it publicly, you will be given a URL, which you can share with anyone. They will then be able to view any of the images you upload to this photo stream.

When you tap 'Next', you will be able to add a comment to the photos you are posting, and then they will be sent. Now, if you tap on 'Photo Stream' in the top toolbar, you will see all of the photo streams you have shared, and all the photo streams that have been shared with you.

Open a photo stream, and an image inside it, and you are able to like it, and also post comments. Anyone who has access to the Photo Stream will be able to see these. You might not want to see the photos other people want to share with you. If that's the case it is possible to turn off photo sharing. To do this go to "Settings", then "Photos & Cameras" and then switch off the "Photo Sharing" button like this.

Camera connection kit

Sometimes you may not want to take photos on your iPad, and instead use a digital camera. If you would like to then import these photos onto your iPad, you will need the iPad Camera Connection Kit from Apple. This allows you to connect a camera with USB, or plug in a SD card, and import the photos onto your iPad.

Connect the appropriate connector to your iPad, then plug in your camera or SD card. If it is not open already, the Photos app will open, and you will see a 'Camera' section in the top toolbar. In this section, all the photos on your camera or SD card will be displayed. You can either import all your photos, or tap on the ones you would like to have on your iPad, then press "Import".

When you press import, a loading icon will appear on the photos or videos that your iPad is importing. When they are imported, a green tick will appear. When the import is complete, you will be asked if you want to delete or keep the photos from your camera or SD card. If you choose to delete them, they will be removed from your camera or card, but not from your iPad. When you are finished, simply remove the camera connection kit.

If this is the first time you have imported photos from a camera, an Events section will have appeared in the top toolbar. Tap on it, and you will see all

the photos you have imported, organised by the date they were taken. In addition to this, two new albums titled 'Last Import' and 'All Imported' will have appeared in the 'Albums' section. You can open these to view your imported photos.

Your photos will also have appeared in the Photos section. You can add these to albums, edit them, and delete them, just like any other photos.

Slide shows

If you would like to share photos with friends, there is a slideshow ability built into the Photos app on your iPad. To use it, open an album containing the photos you would like to display, then tap Slideshow.

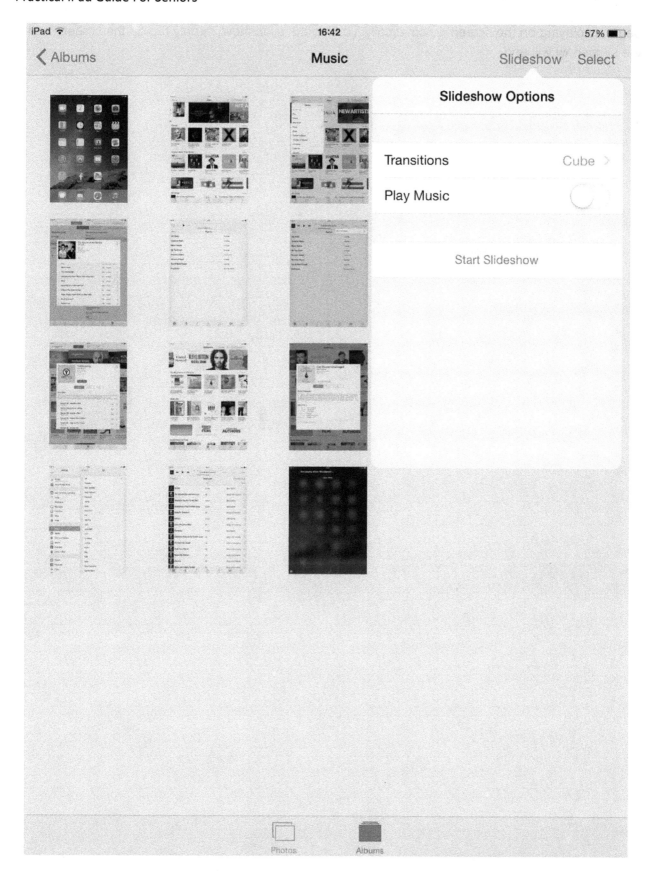

From here you can choose the transition type and turn music on or off. If you turn music on, you can then select a song of your choice to have playing when you view the photos. Unfortunately you can only select one song. When you have done this, tap 'Start Slideshow' to begin. Your photos will begin displaying on the screen automatically.To stop the slideshow, simply tap on the screen, and the slideshow will end.

Taking Pictures with iPad

All iPads that are version 2 and up have in-built cameras on the front and back of the device. To use these, open the Camera app from the Home Screen.

You can tap to focus on a certain object in the scene and adjust the exposure, then press the camera button to take a photo.

There are also more advanced options. You can show a grid when you are taking a photo by tapping 'Options', then turning the switch on. This helps you use the rule of thirds and align your photos correctly. You can also lock exposure and focus by pressing and holding on an object. Now, until you tap on the screen again, the exposure and focus of the camera will remain exactly as they are. To switch to the front camera, tap on this icon. You can switch back again by tapping on it.

The Photo Booth app allows you to apply effects to your camera, live. Open it, and you will be able to see each effect on screen. Tap on one to select it, then tap the camera button to take a photo.

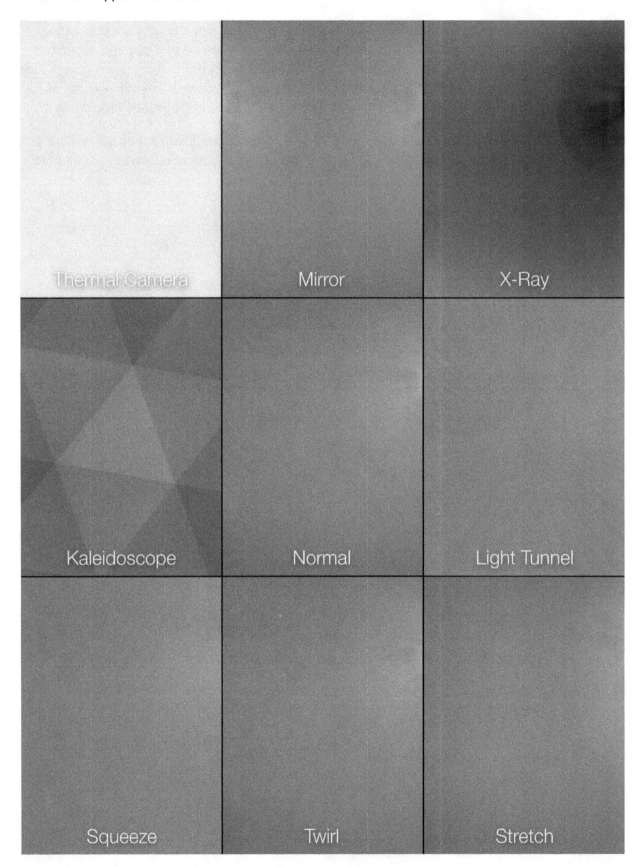

As with the Camera app, you can switch which camera you would like to take the photo from.

Photo Books

It's possible to group your photos together in a photo book that will be printed and sent to you. Go into iPhotos and tap on "Projects". Next tap on "+" and select "Photo Book". Pick a size and a theme, then tap on "Create". You will be given a layout with a toolbar. Choose a page and tap on it like this to browse and add photos. Tap and hold the photo to move it into position. Once you've finished creating your photo book, you'll be given the option to buy it. Tap on "buy" to place your order.

Listening To Music, Podcasts & Audiobooks

iTunes

iTunes is the only way you are able to purchase and download music on your iPad. Music is the app you'll need to listen to it. To begin with, you'll need to open the iTunes store.

From here, you will be taken to the main page. The most popular and newest music will be displayed on here, as well as as the latest offers and discounts,

such as the free single of the week.

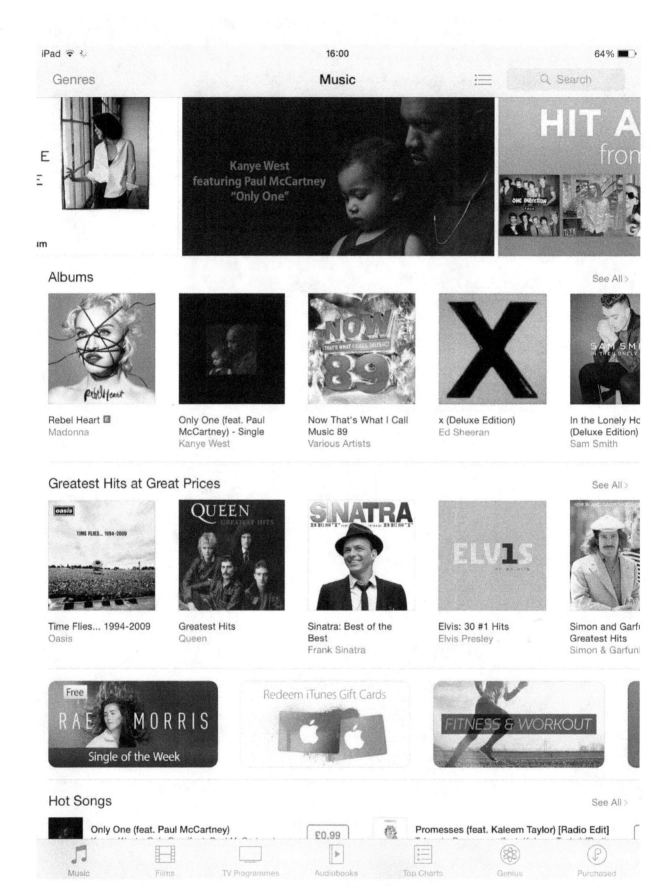

To view music from a certain genre, use the toolbar at the top, and select the genre you are interested in. You will then only be shown relevant results.

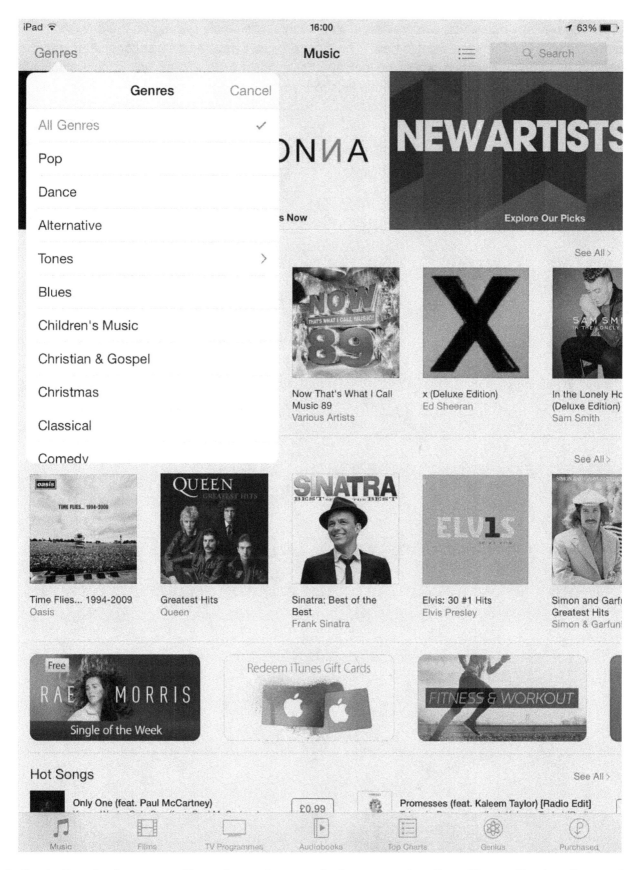

In the bottom toolbar, you will see the various products you can buy from iTunes. To view the music charts, tap on the top charts icon You will then be able to see the current most popular songs and albums. If you want to search for something more specific, tap in the search bar and type in the name of the song, artist, or album that you're looking for.

Before you buy any music you can preview it. You do this by simply pressing on the artwork associated with the song you want to hear. The song previews are about 90 seconds long and they remain playing on your screen, while you look at other things. Music with explicit lyrics will be marked with a red E. When the preview has finished, you will be prompted to buy it. You can either press buy or close the preview.

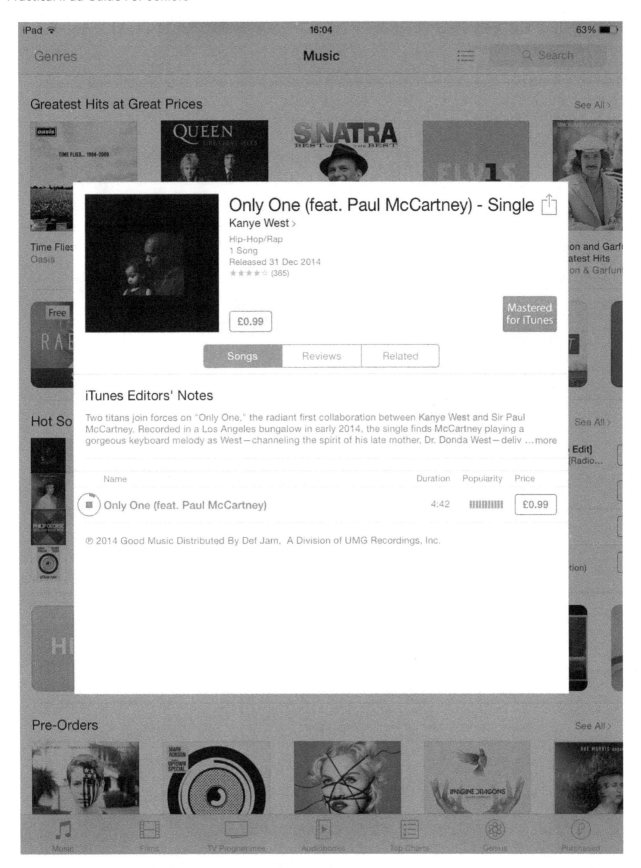

When you find the music you would like to download, tap on the price, then on 'Buy Song'. In order to make the purchase, you will probably be prompted to enter your Apple ID password. The only time you won't have to enter your password is when you've made a purchase just a few minutes previously. If the song is free, you only need to press on the free button for it to download. After pressing buy or free, your song will appear in the downloads section. You can see the progress of your downloads from here.

When your song has downloaded it will appear in the songs section of your 'Purchased' playlist.

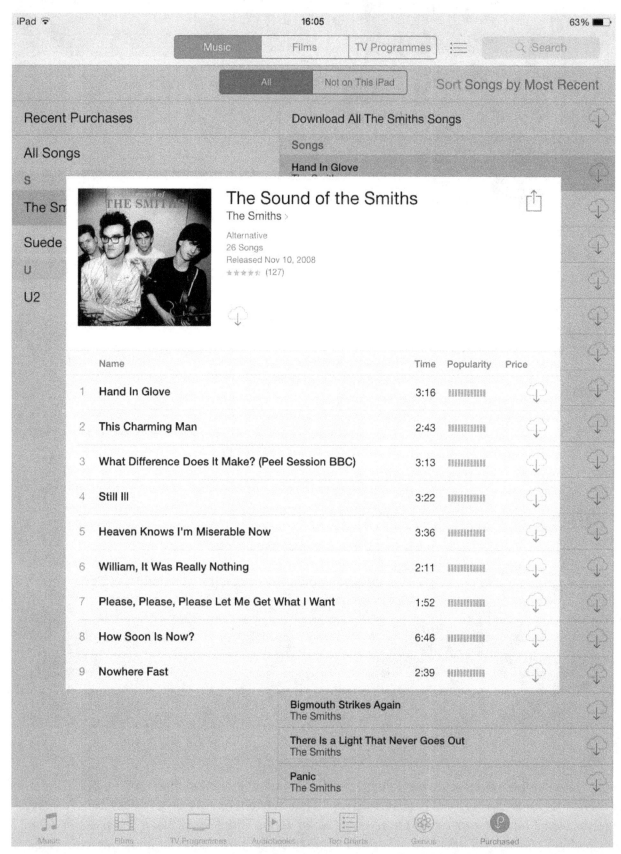

All the music that you purchase can be seen in the purchased playlist and you can re-download purchased items as many times as you'd like. To re-download, go into purchased items and tap the download button.

Transferring music from/to computer

When it comes to syncing music to an iPad, there are a few different options.

The first is to allow iTunes to do the majority of the management. This means that whenever you add a new song to your iTunes library, it will be synced automatically, so you don't have to worry about remembering to do it. To do this, open iTunes on your computer, then plug your iPad in.

You can then select it in the top right and click on Music. Select the 'sync music' checkbox. You can then either sync your entire library, or select certain playlists, artists, albums, and genres. If you select the latter, you will be presented with four boxes. Check all that apply, and any song that falls in one or more of these categories will be added to your iPad.

You also have the options to transfer Music Videos, Voice Memos, and to automatically fill your iPad's free space with music. If you are worried about space, you can also convert music to a lower quality format. This means your music may not sound quite as good, but will take up significantly less room.

If you have unchecked certain songs because you don't listen to them much, you may not want them on your iPad. To make sure this doesn't happen, click on Summary, then tick the box that says 'sync only ticked songs and videos'.

If you don't want iTunes to be in control of what goes on your iPad, you can also manually manage music and video. If you tick the box in the Summary page, all music that has been synced to your iPad will be removed. When you have ticked it, click on "Done", then click and drag any songs you want to be on your iPad.

Your iPad will appear in a panel to the right. Drag the songs on top of it, and they will be transferred. To select multiple songs, click on the first one, press and hold shift, then click on the last one. All songs in between will be selected. You can then release shift, and drag the songs onto your iPad.

To select multiple songs while excluding others, click on the first song you want to transfer, then hold down Control on Windows, and Command on Mac. You can then click on any other songs you would like to transfer. When you are done, release control or command, then drag the songs onto your iPad.

You can also use the buttons at the top, and transfer all music from certain Albums, Playlists, Genres, or by certain Artists. When you have selected all the music you want to transfer – using either method – open the device, then tap Sync, and all of your music will appear on your iPad.

A third possibility is using iCloud to transfer the music. If all your music is stored in the iCloud, tap settings and then iCloud. You'll have to enter your Apple ID. After this, go back to settings and tap on iTunes and App stores in order to enable the Music button. Please note that this method will only transfer music purchased from the iTunes store. You'll have to enable iTunes match (and there is a small fee to use this service) to bring the rest of your music over in this way. However, if all of your music is stored in the iCloud, you will be able to access it from any Apple device.

Playlists

Often there are certain songs that you feel go together well, or you may sometimes want to listen to certain songs in a certain order. To do this, you can create playlists right on your iPad. Open the Music app, then tap on 'Playlists' in the bottom toolbar.

From here you can tap 'New' to create a playlist, which you can name whatever you like.

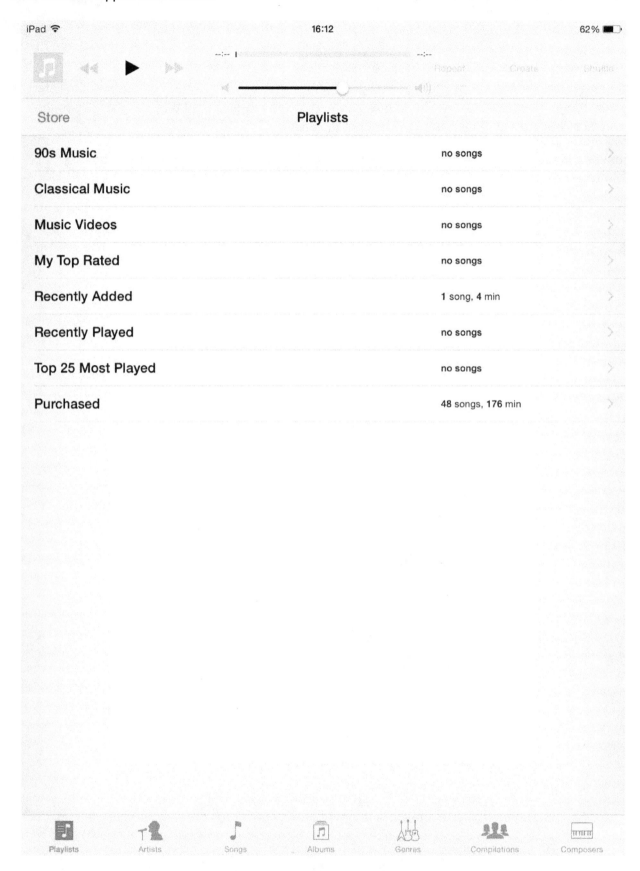

You can then select certain songs to add to your playlist by tapping on the plus arrow. When you have added a song it will turn grey, but if you want it on the playlist multiple times for some reason, you can tap on it again and it will be added.

Tap done, and you will be shown your playlist. You can remove songs by using the red button on the side, and you can rearrange songs using the three lines on the right. When you have finished, tap 'Done'. You can then tap on a song, and the playlist will begin.

If you want to adjust a playlist, tap on the 'Edit' button. You can then rearrange, remove, and add new songs. To delete a playlist, go back to the main playlist page, then press and hold on the playlist. A black circle with a cross will appear. Tap on this and the playlist will be removed permanently.

It's also possible to create a genius playlist on the iPad. A genius playlist is a playlist of songs which you can create automatically by selecting just one song. The rest of the songs will be chosen for you and based on their similarity to the original song. If you don't have enough music in your library, you won't be able to do this.

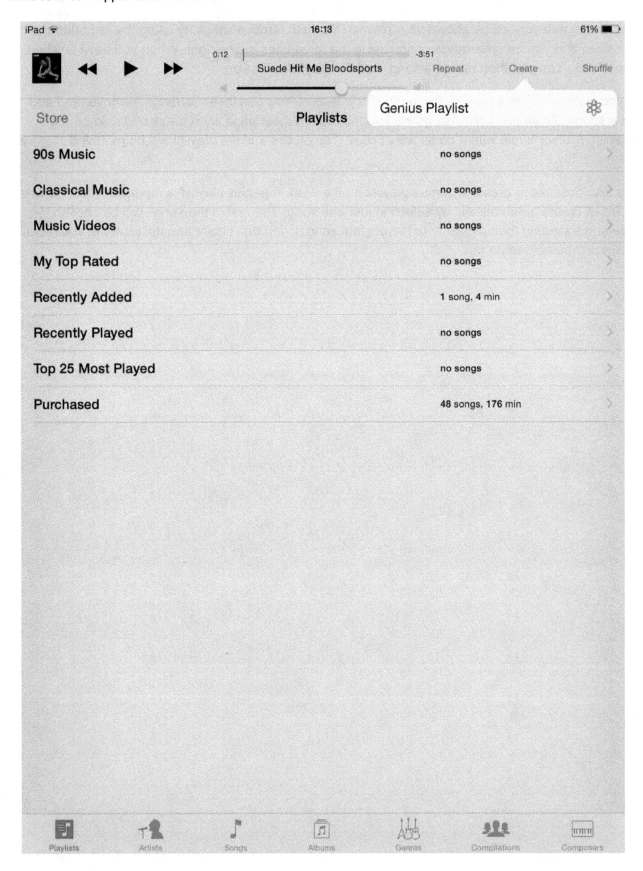

If you have three or more songs in your library, you will also be able to use the shuffle button, which plays the songs in your playlist randomly but in a new order each time

iTunes Radio

iTunes radio is located in the music app. You can create your own iTunes station and share it with your friends, or you can listen to existing iTunes stations and be given the option to purchase any of the songs you hear. Some of the stations are curated by Djs and artists, other stations feature a lot of previews and new releases. Other still provide chart run-downs.

The songs that you listen to on iTunes radio are all saved in your history, so you can go back and see what you listened to. You also have the option to purchase the song from the history. The history can be cleared by pressing the clear button. However, it will erase everything. It's not possible to erase single items

To make your own custom station, press new station, select your genres and add your songs. You can use the edit button to edit your stations. To delete a station press edit and delete. Once you've created it, you'll be able to share the station with others.

You can buy any song you hear on iTunes radio. If the song is playing, click on the price of it to buy it, or if the song has been played previously, you'll need to go into your iTunes radio history, select the song and click on the price displayed there.

Podcasts

Apple made a change in iOS 6 which meant that you have to download a separate Podcasts app for free to play and manage your Podcasts in. Go the the App Store, search Podcasts, and then download the app. When it has finished installing, tap to open it.

iPad 🛜   16:22   61% 🔋

All Categories | All | Audio | Video |

New & Noteworthy   See All >

| Fun Kids at the BAFTA Children's Awards | Hi My Name Is Mark 🄴 | Dear Sugar Radio | NaturalMotion with David Coulthard: Me... | Screen Junkies: M Fights |
| Kids & Family | Music | Society & Culture | Technology | TV & Film |

Fitness   See All >

| YOGAmazing | We Do Science! The Guru Performance... | Ben Greenfield Fitness: Fitness, Fat Loss an... | Yoga Practice Video - Yoga Vidya | The FitCast: Fitnes and Nutrition Podc |
| Alternative Health | Fitness & Nutrition | Fitness & Nutrition | Amateur | Fitness & Nutrition |

 My Podcasts   My Stations   Featured   Top Charts   🔍 Search

--

You will be asked if you want to turn on Auto-Download and if you want to sync your podcasts with your Apple ID. These can be very useful if you have multiple iOS or Mac devices.

To download a podcast, tap on the Store button in the bottom left. You will then be taken to an interface that is very similar to the iTunes store. You will see featured podcasts in all categories by default, but you can also filter them by category using the toolbar at the top.

Audio and video podcasts are available, and you can look at either by tapping on the tab bar at the bottom. If you wish to view the most popular podcasts, you can also tap on Top Charts, and you will see the most popular video and audio podcasts. If you know what you are looking for, you can search for it in the search bar at the top.

When you find the podcast you would like, tap on its cover. You can then either subscribe, or download individual episodes.

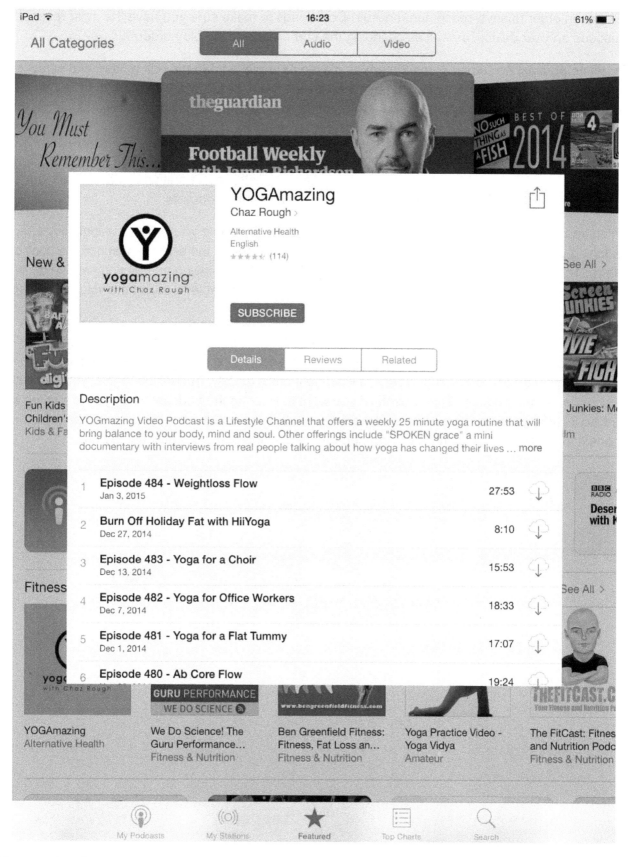

If you subscribe, the most recent episode will appear in your library. You can tap on it to stream, or you can download it if you wish to make it available offline. You can tap 'Add Old Episodes' to download older episodes of the podcast.

The 'Settings' button allows you to turn subscriptions on and off. If it is on, your podcast will automatically update when a new episode becomes available. You can also choose which episodes to keep, in order to save space, turn on Auto-Downloads to make sure you have the most recent episodes on your device, as well as changing the sort order and the play order.

To delete podcast episodes, or mark them as played or unplayed, tap the edit button, and select the podcasts you would like to modify. You can then delete them, or tap 'Mark' to mark them as played or unplayed. If you find a podcast is really interesting, you can share it using the action sheet at the top.

When you are finished modifying or listening to a podcast, tap outside it, and it will disappear. The Podcast app interface also lets you view your podcasts as lists, create stations – which are very similar to Playlists in iTunes – and quickly view the most popular podcasts.

When you have downloaded a podcast, there is a shortcut to enable you to listen to it quickly after switching your device on. Unlock your iPad and swipe upwards on the screen to launch the control centre. The control centre will show you the name of the podcast playing and all you have to do is press on it to listen. While you're in the control centre, you will be able to adjust the volume as well. To close it, swipe downwards.

When you are playing podcasts, as well as being able to play, pause, skip, fast-forward, rewind, and go back, you can jump forward or backward by 15 seconds, scrub through the podcast, and change the speed of a podcast playback to listen to it more quickly. In addition to this, you can set a sleep timer for the podcast. This is useful if you want to listen to the podcast when you are going to bed, so it isn't playing all night. Tap on the clock icon, then select how long you would like the podcast to play before stopping. You are then free to play the podcast whilst drifting off.

Audiobooks

If you prefer having books read to you rather than reading them yourself, you can download audiobooks in iTunes. To do this, open the iTunes app, then tap on Audiobooks in the tab bar. From here you can see a featured page of all genres. You can use the tab bar at the top to filter by genre, or search for a specific book using the search function.

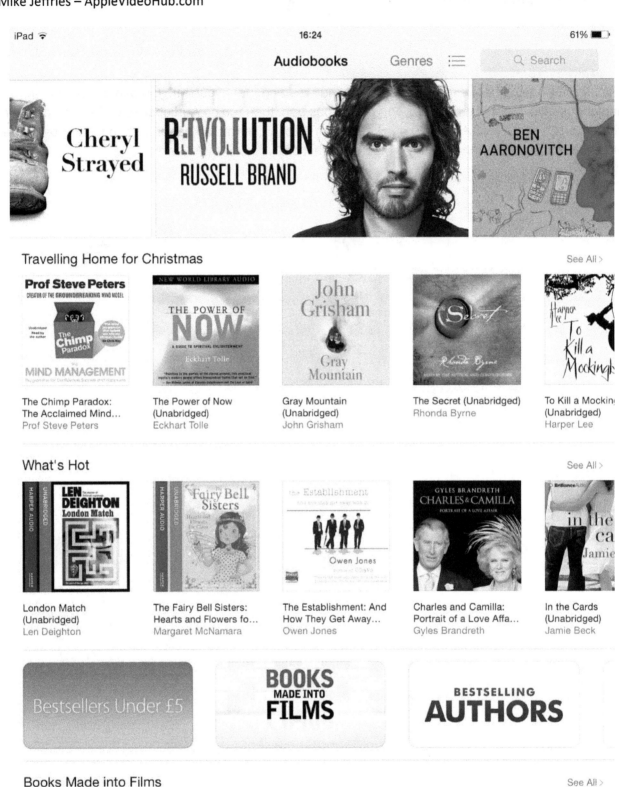

If you do this, you will be shown book, music, film, and TV results, too. To filter this, tap on 'Audiobooks' in the toolbar at the top. You can download a book in the same way you download a song; by tapping on the price, then on buy now. The book will be downloaded to your iPad in the downloads section.

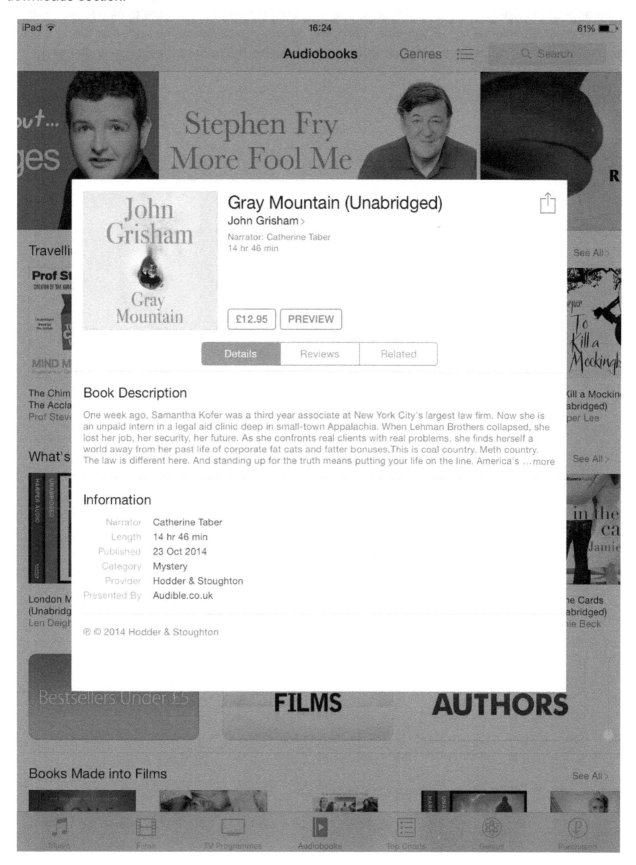

When it has downloaded, you can play it in the Music app. Tap on 'More' in the bottom toolbar, then on Audiobooks. You will then be able to play your book. It's worth mentioning two new buttons which appear in Audiobooks. One of them is the skip button. You are now able to skip forwards by 15 seconds or backwards by 15 seconds. The other allows you to adjust the speed at which it plays back to you. For an optimum audiobook listening experience, make sure the EQ settings are on Spoken word.

Audio Controls

Before you control your sounds, you'll need to find them! In the Music app, there is a toolbar along the bottom of the screen, which allows you to browse your music library by album, artist, composer or compilation. All your music can be found in here. If you want to edit these tabs, you can, simply by pressing the more tab and then edit. When you've finished dragging the icons around, tap done.

There are different ways of controlling your music on the iPad. Firstly, there are the controls in the Music app. These allow you to Pause, Play, skip, fast forward, rewind, and go back.

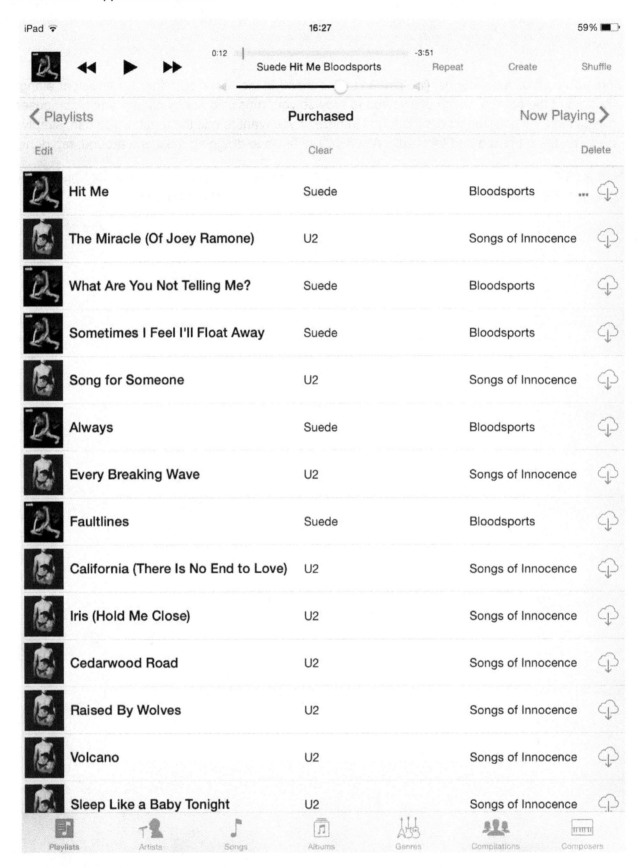

You can also use these controls to skim through a song, adjust the volume, and turn shuffle on and off, as well as adjusting the volume. You can change how fast you move forwards and backwards through the song by dragging your finger up towards the artwork. There are 4 speeds available.

The volume slider is used to control the volume of the music app, but not your device. You will need to press the settings icon on your homescreen and the sound button to alter this. If you need it, it's possible to set a music volume limit. This may be useful if your children use your iPad.

The looping function lets you make sure your music plays constantly. Tap it once, and the playlist or album you are currently in will loop forever. If you tap it again, the current song will repeat. Tap it once more to turn looping off. If you are in another app, you don't have to switch to the Music

app to control your music. Open the multitasking bar by double tapping the home button or swiping up with four fingers, then swipe to the left. From here you can play and pause your music, as well as skipping, fast-forwarding, rewinding, and going back a song. The slider allows you to change the volume, and there is a button to open the Music app.

The final way of controlling music is in the lock screen. Double tap the home button, and you will be given the same set of controls as in the multitasking bar, minus the shortcut to the Music app. The lock screen will also display the album artwork of the current song you are playing. You will still be able to make the song pause, play, move backwards and forwards as well as control the volume.

EQ settings

Given the different environments in which we listen to music, it's worth knowing how to change the EQ settings in order to provide you with best listening experience regardless of where you are, or what's going on around you. You need the EQ settings to help you adjust sound frequencies and enable you to hear your music better even when there is a lot of background noise.

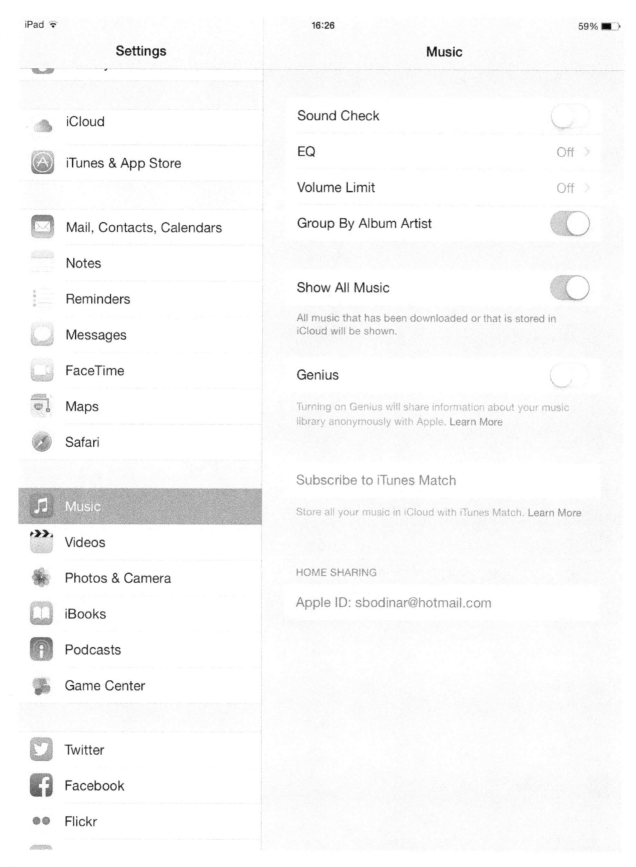

To adjust your EQ settings, press settings on the homescreen and tap on EQ. There are 23 preset equalizer settings to choose from and the changes you make will apply to all songs you play. It is possible to adjust EQ settings for individual songs via the iTunes app.

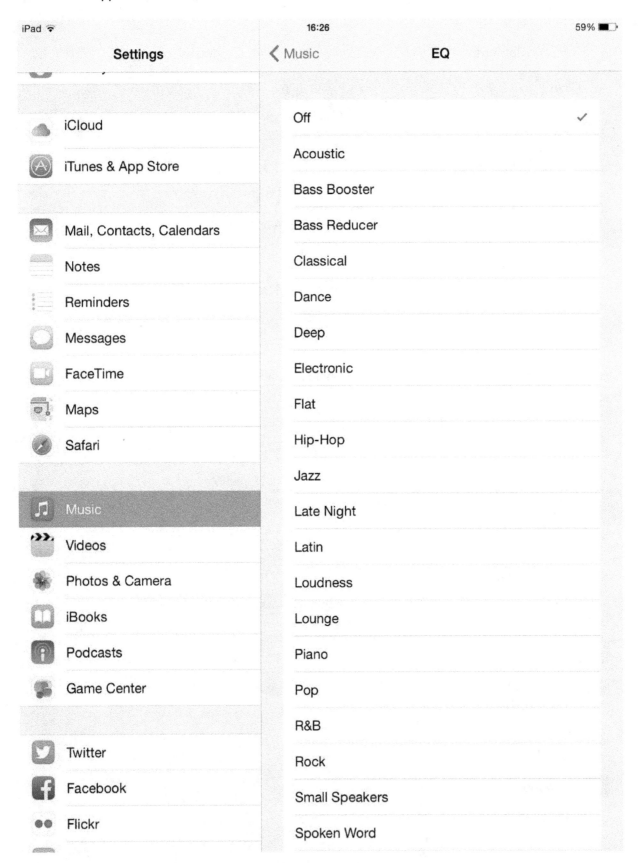

Siri

For the visually impaired, Siri is the Apple's voice activation system. You can use Siri with the Music app, simply by saying aloud the name of the song you want to hear

Siri commands for the music app include

"Play"

"Pause"

"Skip"

You can say also say the name of the song, album or artist after each of these

To hide the music controls, simply double tap the home button again. And that is how you control your music on the iPad.

Fun with Apps

The App Store

The App Store is where you download apps for your iPad. It's the only way you can get new apps for your device and new ones are released daily. When you open it, you will be presented with a page of featured apps. This page is updated regularly.

If you see an app which looks interesting, tap on it, and a preview will appear, in which you you will be able to see a description of the app, its ratings and its reviews.

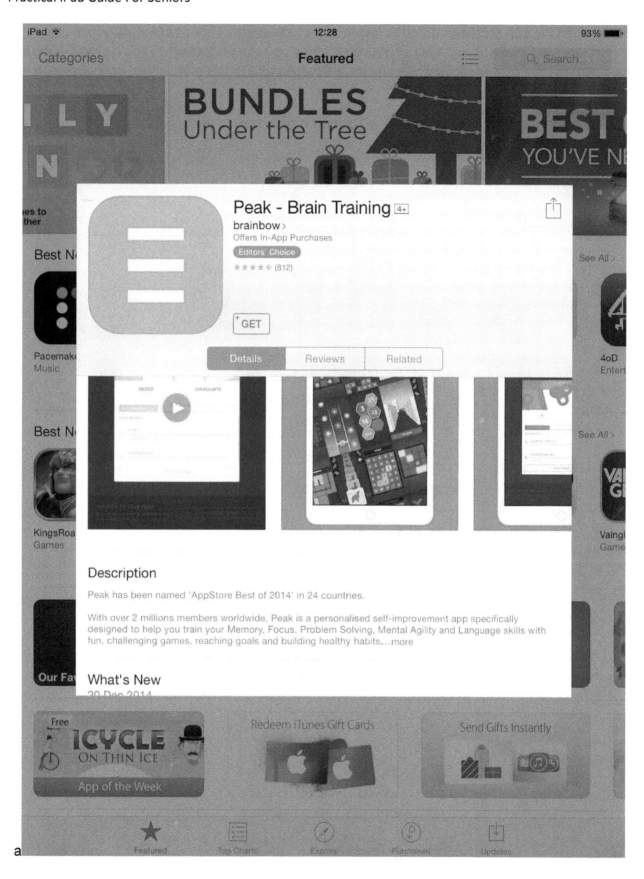

Bear in mind that without tapping on an app its name may be shortened. Tapping on it will display the full name. The apps are also given a user rating. This has been provided by people who have downloaded the app and been asked to rate it. As for reviews, this button will allow you to like a specific app on Facebook and read what users of the app have said about it. You can also submit your own reviews here for apps which you have downloaded. I'll talk more about writing reviews in a minute.

Many apps are free, but ones that aren't will display a price next to the app icon.

To download a paid app, tap on the price, then tap "Buy App". You will need to input your Apple ID.

For a free app, tap on the button which says "Free" then tap "Install App".

Your app will begin downloading, and appear on your homescreen.

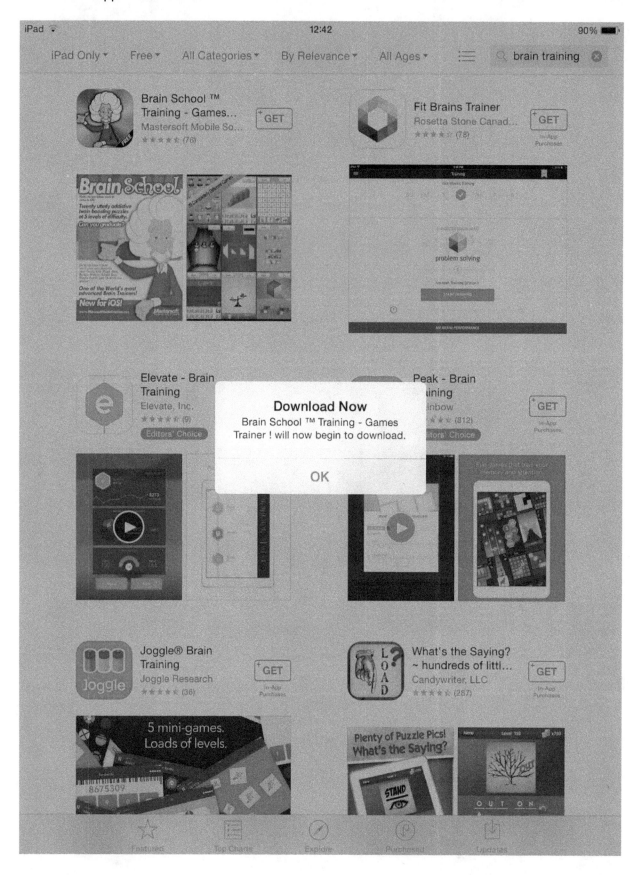

If you're going to use a gift card for the purchase, you'll need to tap on the "Redeem" button here and type in your Apple ID and password

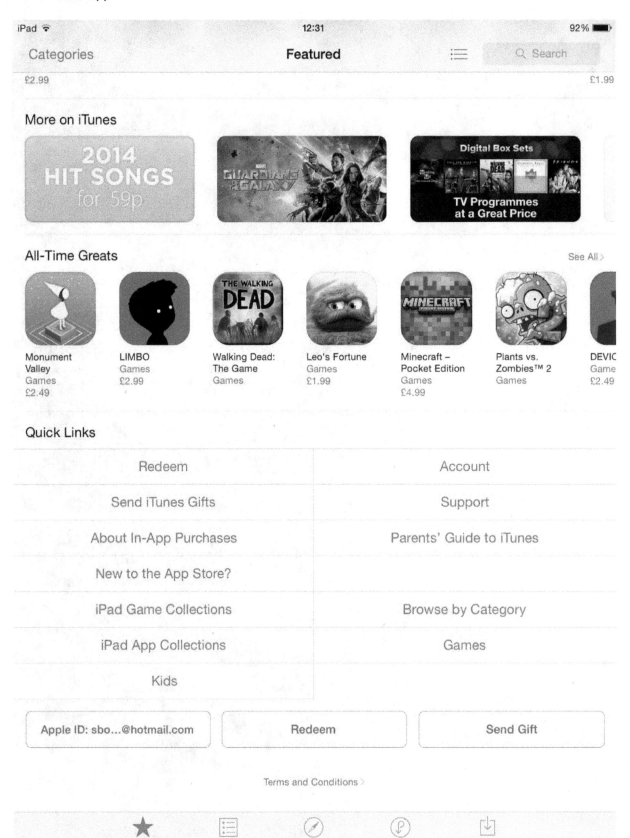

Apps you have previously purchased with your iTunes account will display an Install button, regardless of whether they are paid or free. You can download these applications again as many times as you like.

To view all the apps you have ever purchased, tap on "Purchased" at the bottom. You can choose to view either all the apps you have ever purchased, or just ones that aren't on your iPad. You can also sort the apps by recency, or by name. Tap on the iCloud icon to install an app for free.

The App Store contains a wealth of interesting apps, but sometimes it can be difficult to find ones that interest you. The featured section shows you some of the latest and best apps available, as well as some topical categories such as Christmas apps.

To discover apps, you can also look in specific categories. To do this, tap on one of the categories at the top, or tap on More to view a complete list of categories.

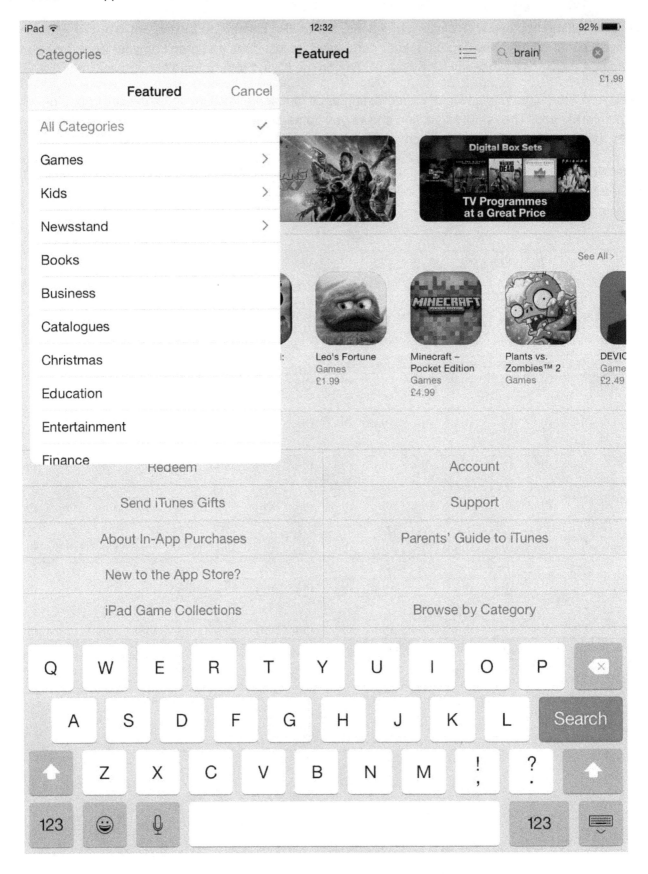

When you have selected a category, you will see apps from that category listed in four sections: "New", "What's Hot", "Paid", and "Free". You can swipe to the right to see a few more apps in these sections, or press "See All" to view all of them.

Apple also groups similar apps together in collections to help you search. The collections are stored within the app categories. New collections are added frequently.

We've sifted through hundreds of thousands of apps to create these indispensable collections. Whatever you do with your iPhone, iPad or iPod touch—shopping, watching films, editing photos and beyond—you'll find apps that work smartly and beautifully.

This one-stop shop for new customers is tailored to provide a core set of indispensable apps.

Download iBooks, Podcasts, GarageBand, iPhoto, iMovie, Find My iPhone, Pages, iTunes U, Remote and more.

Whether they're counting critters or belting out songs, kids will love this collection of engaging educational apps.

If you're visiting Newsstand for the first time, start with our hand-picked assortment of stunning titles and popular magazines.

Find all our favourite apps and games in one place—from innovative time-savers to extraordinary puzzlers.

Handle investments, bank accounts, taxes, shares and bills with this collection of excellent finance apps.

From tracking stats to watching live matches, this collection has all the apps you need to support your team.

Perfect for bloggers and novelists alike, these apps help with manuscripts, invoicing, enjoying coffee breaks and more.

From major retailers to deal-finders, list-makers and barcode scanners, these apps help you shop better.

In the Top Charts section you can see the most-downloaded paid and free apps, in order of popularity. The Top Charts can also be sorted by category.

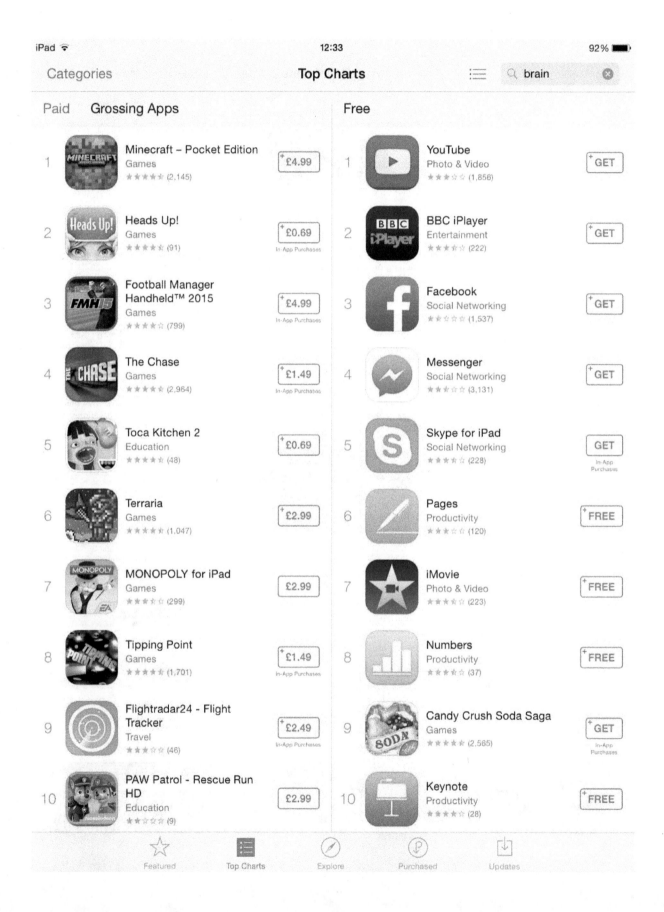

If your location services are switched on, you'll have the option to search for local apps known as "Near me" and you'll be shown apps that are popular in your geographical area.

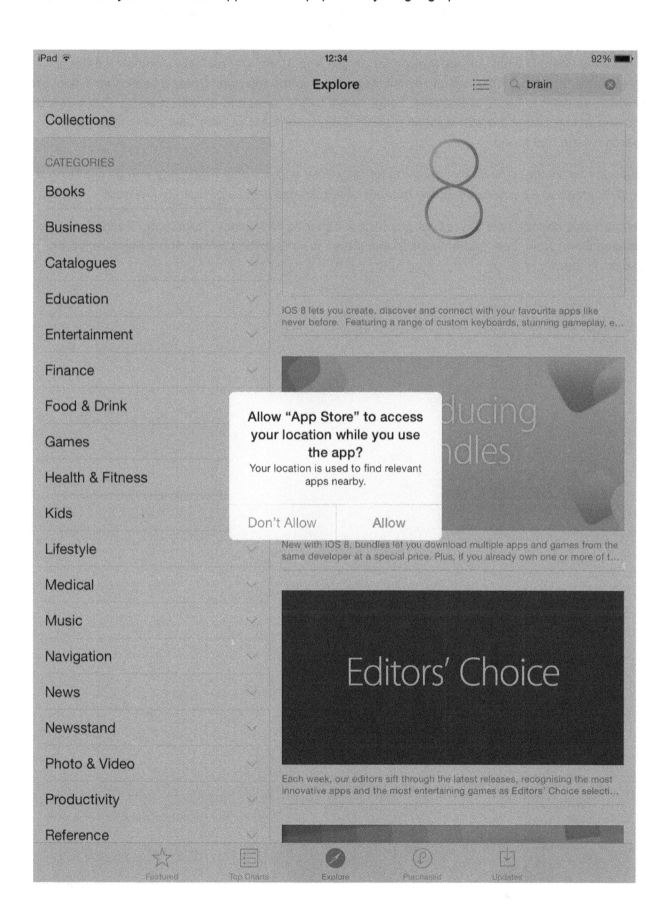

When you find an app you want to bookmark with a view to purchasing it at a later date, tap on the app and then tap on "add to wishlist". Your wishlist can be seen on every page of the app store and you can buy items directly from it. Press "done" when you've finished viewing the wishlist to return to the app store.

If you know roughly what you are looking for on the App Store, you can use the search function. To do so, open the App Store, then tap on the search bar in the top right. Enter a search term relevant to what you want to find. For example, I might want to find an app to do with reading. Press search, and you will be presented with a list of apps. In the top right you will see how many apps your search results has found.

You can narrow these down by searching for only Free apps or only Paid apps and by choosing a certain category. As you can see, the number of results has been significantly lowered.

You can also change how the results are sorted, either by:Relevance, Popularity, Ratings, or Release Date. Now, I can tap on apps to see if they are interesting to me, and if they are, I can download them.

Updating Apps

It's important to keep apps updated with the latest version. This will prevent some common app problems from occurring. You can set your iPad to update apps automatically by going into settings, then iTunes & App store, then updates, or, if you prefer, you can do update each app manually.

If apps on your iPad require updates, the App Store icon will display a badge. Open the app store then tap on updates to see what apps are ready to update. Next to the app icon will be text letting you know what the update will bring. Make sure you read this carefully. You can update apps individually by pressing Update, or update all of them by tapping "Update All".When you tap update, it will download, and you will see a loading bar. When it has finished, you can open the app, and enjoy the app in its updated form.

iPad 📶   12:38   91% 🔋

Settings	iTunes & App Store

Settings

- ✈️ Airplane Mode ⚪
- 📶 Wi-Fi   network123
- ✳️ Bluetooth   Off

- 🔲 Notifications
- 🎛️ Control Centre
- 🌙 Do Not Disturb

- ⚙️ General
- 🔤 Display & Brightness
- 🌼 Wallpaper
- 🔊 Sounds
- 🔒 Passcode
- ✋ Privacy

- ☁️ iCloud
- Ⓐ **iTunes & App Store**

- ✉️ Mail, Contacts, Calendars
- 📝 Notes
- 📋 Reminders
- 💬 Messages

iTunes & App Store

Apple ID:

SHOW ALL

Music ⚪

Videos ⚪

Show all store purchases and iTunes Match uploads in your music and video libraries, even if they have not been downloaded to this iPad.

Subscribe to iTunes Match

Store all your music in iCloud with iTunes Match. Learn more...

AUTOMATIC DOWNLOADS

🎵 Music ⚪

Ⓐ Apps ⚪

📖 Books ⚪

Ⓐ Updates ⚪

Automatically download new purchases (including free) made on other devices.

SUGGESTED APPS

My Apps ⚪

App Store ⚪

Show installed apps or App Store suggestions for apps relevant to your current location, on the Lock screen and in the app switcher.

Deleting Apps

If you decide that an app is no longer, or never was, useful to you, you can remove it from your iPad.

Before you do this, you need to remember that while you can reinstall the app, the app's data will be permanently removed from your iPad, so be sure to back up anything useful beforehand.

To delete an app, go to your homescreen, then press and hold on any app until the apps begin to jiggle. Find the app you would like to delete, then tap on the black cross in the a white circle on the top left of the icon. You will be asked to confirm your deletion, then the app will be instantly removed from your iPad. Deleting apps that aren't useful is a good way to save storage space, and keep your iPad's home screen organised.

Reviewing Apps

Sometimes you may come across an app that you think is too good for anyone not to download, or one that is so terrible that other people should avoid it.

A way to get your opinion heard is by leaving a review in the App Store.

To do this, open the App Store, then search for the app you would like to review. Tap on its icon, then tap on Ratings and Reviews.

Here you have a few options. You can either just give it a rating out of five, or write a more detailed review. If you have added a Facebook account, you can also like the app on Facebook.

Reviewing Apps

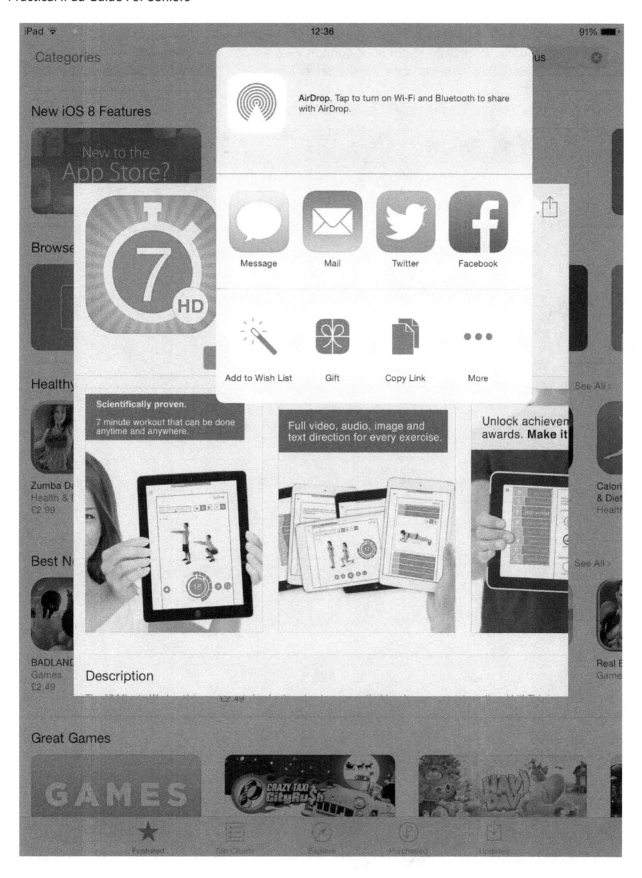

To write a detailed review, tap on "Write a Review". You will have to enter your password, and if you have never left a review on the App Store before, you will be asked to enter a username, which will be displayed publicly on the App Store.

When you have done this, you can choose how many stars you want to rate the app, and enter a title. If you feel the title is enough to get your point of view across, you can leave it at that, but if you want to enter more details, you can do so in the review box.

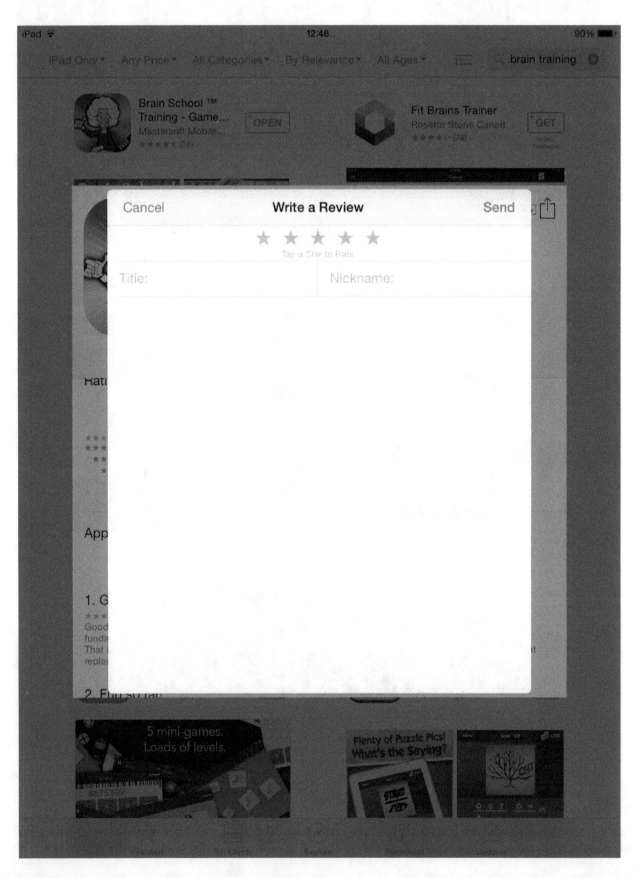

When you are finished, tap submit, and your review will be sent to Apple. It will not appear in the app review immediately, as it requires moderation. If you decide at any point you want to change your review, for example, if the app was updated and the issues you had been experiencing were fixed, you can change your review.

To do this, simply find the app again in the App Store, then tap on "Write a Review". Your old review will appear, and you can edit it and then submit it.

Adding positive reviews also helps developers, and can result in more frequent and better quality updates from them.

Managing Apple ID

Your Apple ID is what you use to purchase Apps, Music, Videos, and Books on your iPad. To view or edit your account information, open either iTunes

or the App Store, tap on the Featured tab, then scroll down to the bottom. Here, you will see your Apple ID in the bottom left.

Tap on this button, the tap on View Apple ID. You will be asked to enter your password, and then you can view your information.

Managing Apple ID

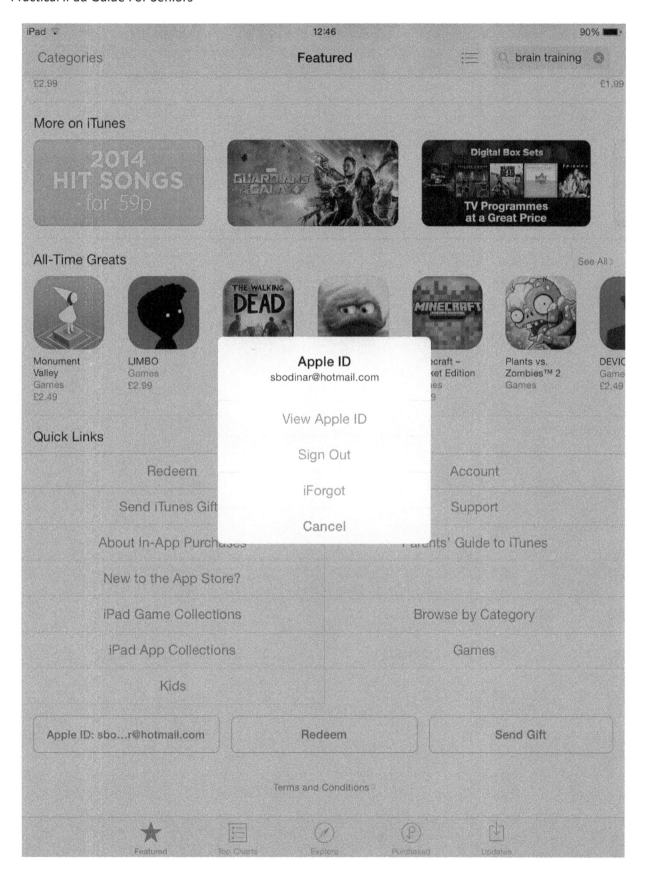

Tap on Apple ID to alter your email and password, "Payment Information" to change which card you use to pay for things, and "Country and Region" to change what content you are shown in the stores.

In addition to this, you can manage what alerts you receive from iTunes and the App Store. Turn the switch on to receive email alerts that are relevant to what you have previously downloaded.

Reading Books

Installing iBooks

The iPad is great for reading books, but to do so, you will need an eBook reader. Apple makes their own one for the iPad, called iBooks. To download iBooks, open the App Store, then search for iBooks. Tap on install and download it. You'll need to type in your Apple ID and password. If you have books are stored on the iCloud, you'll simply need to sign in with your Apple ID to access your iCloud account.

Sync Books from PC

iBooks is the app you'll need for reading your books but the iTunes is the app you'll need for buying them. If you have eBooks or PDFs on your computer, and want to add them to your iPad, you can do so through iTunes.

If the book you want to transfer is not already in your iTunes library, add it by pressing "File" and then "Add to Library" or by dragging it into iTunes. Note: iBooks will only accept eBooks in the ePub format. Once you have imported the file, connect your iPad to the computer. Click on iPad in the right, then on Books. If it isn't already ticked, tick the box next to "Sync Books". You can either sync all your books, or only selected books. If you select the latter option, you will be able to tick certain books in order for them to be synced. When you are done, press "Apply", and the books will be appear in iBooks.

An alternative method is to plug your iPad into your MAC and open iTunes. If you then click on the book you want to transfer, hold it and drag it either to the extreme left or right of the screen, a symbol for your iPad will show up and you will be able to drag the desired book into your iPad. When it highlights, the book has been transferred.

Buying and Downloading Books from iTunes

The easiest way to get books onto your iPad is through the iBookstore. The process is very similar to buying media from iTunes. To access the iBookstore, open iBooks, then tap on "Store". The bookshelf will flip, and you will be in the store. From here, you can see featured books, top charts and top authors.

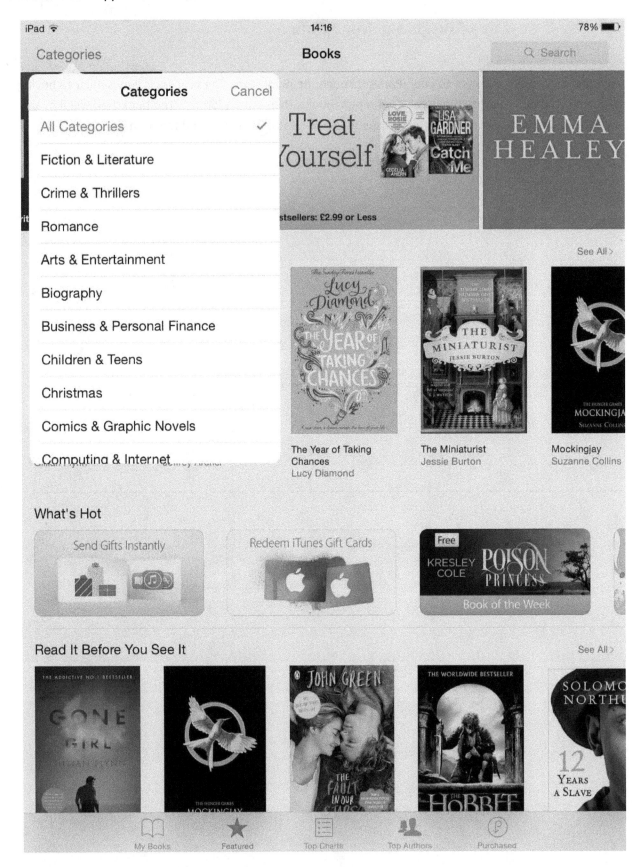

You can also search for titles and authors in the search bar. To see a list of book genres and search this way, tap in the category box. For example, you could search for the author John Green, and see all the books he has written. If you like the look of a certain book, tap on the cover and you will be able to see a description and read reviews. If you are still unsure, you can download a sample of the book for free. Simply tap the "Get Sample" button.

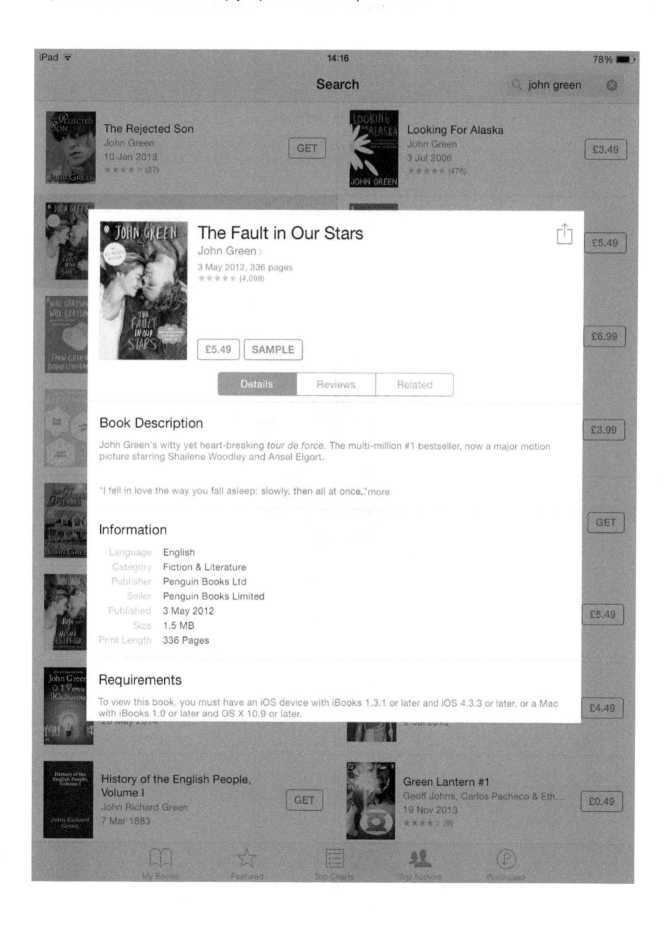

When you get to the end of the sample, you will be given the option of purchasing the complete book.

Continue Reading:

The Fault in Our Stars

John Green

£5.49

Alternatively, you can buy the book in the iBookstore by tapping on the price, tapping buy, then entering your password. The book will download and appear on your shelf. If you don't want to buy the book, tap anywhere outside the window.

Reading a Book

To begin reading a book, tap on its cover in iBooks. This is what your bookshelf looks like:

Just as with an ordinary book, you can turn the page by pulling its corner. In addition to this, you can change pages by swiping backwards and forwards, or tapping on either side of the book.

To delete a book that appears on your bookshelf, tap on edit, then the book itself before finally pressing delete.

In portrait, iBooks displays one page at a time. If you prefer, you can rotate the iPad to landscape, to see two pages at a time, which looks more like an ordinary book.

iBooks also makes it easy to change the format of a book to suit your reading habits. To do this, tap once in the center of the book to make the toolbars appear. In the top right are two letter A's. Tap on them to alter screen brightness, font size, change the font face, and alter the theme.

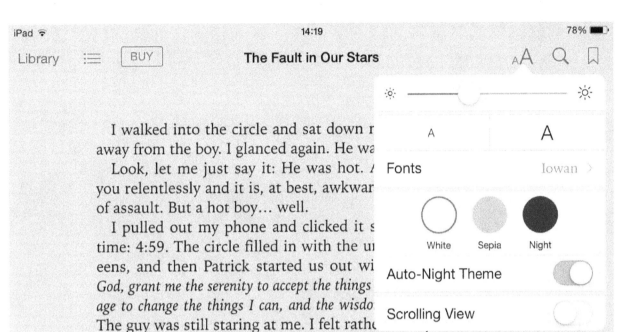

You will have a choice of three themes. They are black writing on a white background which is is called "normal", there's sepia, which is a softer black on an off-white background and the third is a night theme, which is less bright and makes the iPad easier to read in reduced light. It consists of grey writing on a black background.

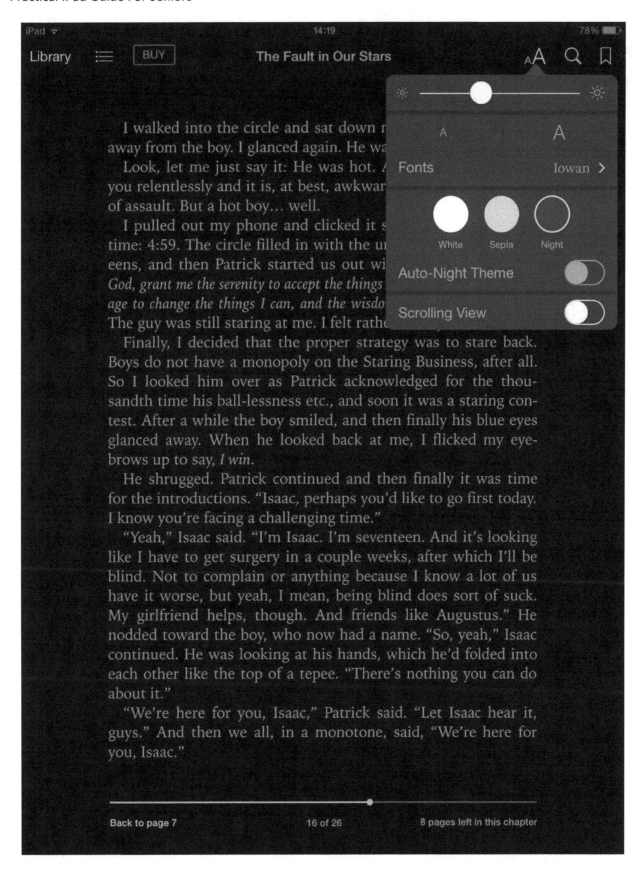

As well as a choice of themes, you are able to choose from a number of different page layouts. Choose from full page, book, or a layout that allows you to read by scrolling.

When you have the book set up how you want it, you're ready to read. Whenever you close and open a book, iBooks remember your last place, and it will automatically open there. However, you can use the bar at the bottom to quickly skim through the book, or tap on this icon in the top left, to quickly skip to chapters.

To search for specific words or phrases, you can use the search bar to find all occurrences in the book. Tap on one of the results to navigate to that point.

If you find a word that you don't understand, double tap it, then press "Define", and a dictionary definition will appear in a popup.

Practical iPad Guide For Seniors

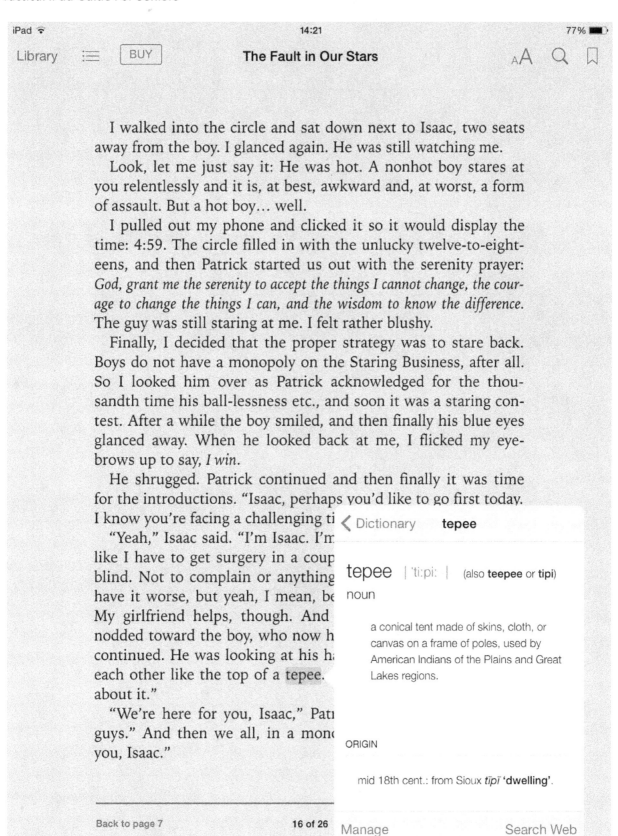

I walked into the circle and sat down next to Isaac, two seats away from the boy. I glanced again. He was still watching me.

Look, let me just say it: He was hot. A nonhot boy stares at you relentlessly and it is, at best, awkward and, at worst, a form of assault. But a hot boy... well.

I pulled out my phone and clicked it so it would display the time: 4:59. The circle filled in with the unlucky twelve-to-eighteens, and then Patrick started us out with the serenity prayer: *God, grant me the serenity to accept the things I cannot change, the courage to change the things I can, and the wisdom to know the difference.* The guy was still staring at me. I felt rather blushy.

Finally, I decided that the proper strategy was to stare back. Boys do not have a monopoly on the Staring Business, after all. So I looked him over as Patrick acknowledged for the thousandth time his ball-lessness etc., and soon it was a staring contest. After a while the boy smiled, and then finally his blue eyes glanced away. When he looked back at me, I flicked my eyebrows up to say, *I win.*

He shrugged. Patrick continued and then finally it was time for the introductions. "Isaac, perhaps you'd like to go first today. I know you're facing a challenging ti

"Yeah," Isaac said. "I'm Isaac. I'm

like I have to get surgery in a coup

blind. Not to complain or anything

have it worse, but yeah, I mean, be

My girlfriend helps, though. And

nodded toward the boy, who now h

continued. He was looking at his ha

each other like the top of a tepee.

about it."

"We're here for you, Isaac," Pat

guys." And then we all, in a mono

you, Isaac."

< Dictionary   **tepee**

tepee | ˈtiːpiː | (also **teepee** or **tipi**)

noun

> a conical tent made of skins, cloth, or canvas on a frame of poles, used by American Indians of the Plains and Great Lakes regions.

ORIGIN

mid 18th cent.: from Sioux *tipi* 'dwelling'.

If a definition isn't available, you will be given the option to search the wider internet for a meaning.

Taking book notes

A useful feature of iBooks is the ability to take notes and highlight passages. To highlight text, press and hold at the start of the passage you would like to highlight, then drag your finger to the end of it.

I walked into the circle and sat down next to Isaac, two seats away from the boy. I glanced again. He was still watching me.

Look, let me just say it: He was hot. A nonhot boy stares at you relentlessly and it is, at best, awkward and, at worst, a form of assault. But a hot boy... well.

I pulled out my phone and clicked it so it would display the time: 4:59. The circle filled in with the unlucky twelve-to-eighteens, and then Patrick started us out with the serenity prayer: *God, grant me the serenity to accept the things I cannot change, the courage to change the things I can, and the wisdom to know the difference.* The guy was still staring at me. I felt rather blushy.

Finally, I decided that the proper strategy was to stare back. Boys do not have a monopoly on the Staring Business, after all. So I looked him over as Patrick acknowledged for the thousandth time his ball-lessness etc., and soon it was a staring contest. After a while the boy smiled, and then finally his blue eyes glanced ⚪ ⚪ ⚪ ⚪ ⚪ Ⓐ 🗑 ⬜ ＞ ny eyebrows up to say, *I win.*

He shrugged. Patrick continued and then finally it was time for the introductions. "Isaac, perhaps you'd like to go first today. I know you're facing a challenging time."

"Yeah," Isaac said. "I'm Isaac. I'm seventeen. And it's looking like I have to get surgery in a couple weeks, after which I'll be blind. Not to complain or anything because I know a lot of us have it worse, but yeah, I mean, being blind does sort of suck. My girlfriend helps, though. And friends like Augustus." He nodded toward the boy, who now had a name. "So, yeah," Isaac continued. He was looking at his hands, which he'd folded into each other like the top of a tepee. "There's nothing you can do about it."

"We're here for you, Isaac," Patrick said. "Let Isaac hear it, guys." And then we all, in a monotone, said, "We're here for you, Isaac."

You can then tap on the highlight, and tap on this icon to change the colour of it. Your highlighting will be saved automatically. To remove the highlight, tap on the white circle with a red line through it. The next time you highlight a passage, it will automatically be in the colour you last used. You can also add notes to passages. To do this, tap on a highlight, then press this icon. A note will appear, in which you can enter text.

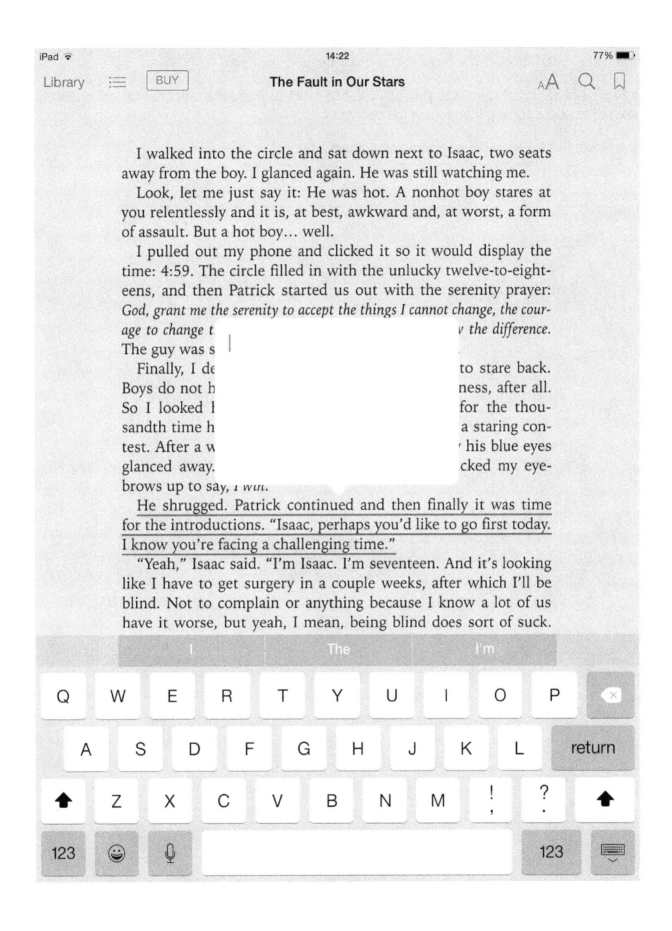

iPad 📶   14:22   77% 🔋

Library ☰ [BUY]   **The Fault in Our Stars**   AA Q 🔖

I walked into the circle and sat down next to Isaac, two seats away from the boy. I glanced again. He was still watching me.

Look, let me just say it: He was hot. A nonhot boy stares at you relentlessly and it is, at best, awkward and, at worst, a form of assault. But a hot boy... well.

I pulled out my phone and clicked it so it would display the time: 4:59. The circle filled in with the unlucky twelve-to-eighteens, and then Patrick started us out with the serenity prayer: *God, grant me the serenity to accept the things I cannot change, the courage to change t   v the difference.* The guy was s

Finally, I de   to stare back. Boys do not h   ness, after all. So I looked l   for the thousandth time h   a staring contest. After a w   his blue eyes glanced away.   cked my eyebrows up to say, *I win.*

He shrugged. Patrick continued and then finally it was time for the introductions. "Isaac, perhaps you'd like to go first today. I know you're facing a challenging time."

"Yeah," Isaac said. "I'm Isaac. I'm seventeen. And it's looking like I have to get surgery in a couple weeks, after which I'll be blind. Not to complain or anything because I know a lot of us have it worse, but yeah, I mean, being blind does sort of suck.

When you are done, simply tap anywhere on the screen to dismiss it. Your note will appear on the right, and you can tap on it to view and edit it.

If you find a passage particularly interesting, you can also share it. To do this, tap on a piece of text you have highlighted, and press the share icon. From here you can send it in an email, message it to someone, post it to twitter or facebook, or copy it to your clipboard.

If a page is of particular interest to you, you can bookmark it. To do this, tap once on the screen to make the toolbars appear, then tap on the bookmark.

If you would like to remove it, simply tap on it again.

Isaac was laughing, but Patrick raised a chastening finger and said, "Augustus, please. Let's return to *you* and *your* struggles. You said you fear oblivion?"

"I did," Augustus answered.

Patrick seemed lost. "Would, uh, would anyone like to speak to that?"

I hadn't been in proper school in three years. My parents were my two best friends. My third best friend was an author who did not know I existed. I was a fairly shy person—not the hand-raising type.

And yet, just this once, I decided to speak. I half raised my hand and Patrick, his delight evident, immediately said, "Hazel!" I was, I'm sure he assumed, opening up. Becoming Part Of The Group.

I looked over at Augustus Waters, who looked back at me. You could almost see through his eyes they were so blue. "There will come a time," I said, "when all of us are dead. All of us. There will come a time when there are no human beings remaining to remember that anyone ever existed or that our species ever did anything. There will be no one left to remember Aristotle or Cleopatra, let alone you. Everything that we did and built and wrote and thought and discovered will be forgotten and all of this"—I gestured encompassingly—"will have been for naught. Maybe that time is coming soon and maybe it is millions of years away, but even if we survive the collapse of our sun, we will not survive forever. There was time before organisms experienced consciousness, and there will be time after. And if the inevitability of human oblivion worries you, I encourage you to ignore it. God knows that's what everyone else does."

I'd learned this from my aforementioned third best friend, Peter Van Houten, the reclusive author of *An Imperial Affliction*, the book that was as close a thing as I had to a Bible. Peter Van Houten was the only person I'd ever come across who seemed

To review all the bookmarks, highlights, and notes you have made, tap on this icon. You can then tap on bookmarks to see where all your bookmarks have been placed, and on notes to see the notes you have made.

Tap the share button in the top right to share the book with someone, or to edit your notes. If you select "Edit Notes" you will be able to select notes you have made, and delete them, or share them via email.

Reading PDFs

As well as being good for reading books, iBooks makes a great PDF reader. When you find a PDF you want to read, your iPad will ask you if you want to open it in iBooks.

iPad 🔊   14:34   ◀ 75% ▆

🔒 s3.amazonaws.com

Open in "iBooks"

When you have added a PDF to iBooks, either through iTunes, Safari, or another app, select the PDF collection in iBooks, then tap on the PDF you wish to view. It's worth noting that if a PDF is small enough you will also be able to email it to yourself, in order to transfer it to your iPad. To download it, go into your Mail app, select the email you have sent and tap and hold on the attachment. You will be given the option to open it in iBooks. Tap on it to transfer it.

You can swipe left or right to navigate the PDF, use the small icons in the bottom toolbar to quickly scan through it, or tap on this icon in the top toolbar to view all the pages laid out, and quickly skip to one.

You can also change the brightness of the screen to make reading more comfortable, search the PDF for certain words or phrases, bookmark useful pages, or tap on the share icon to email or print the PDF.You can pinch to zoom in on sections of the PDF, making it easier to read small text. Links will also work in PDFs, either linking to pages in the document, or to websites. To follow a link, simply tap on it once.

Organizing your Bookshelf

If you have a lot of books on the iPad, your shelf can become quite cluttered. It is possible to press and hold on a book, then drag it, to rearrange your books, but this offers only a certain level of organisation. For better organisation of books, you can use collections. To create a new collection, tap on "Collections" in the top toolbar, then tap "New". Enter a title, then tap anywhere else on the screen to hide the popup.

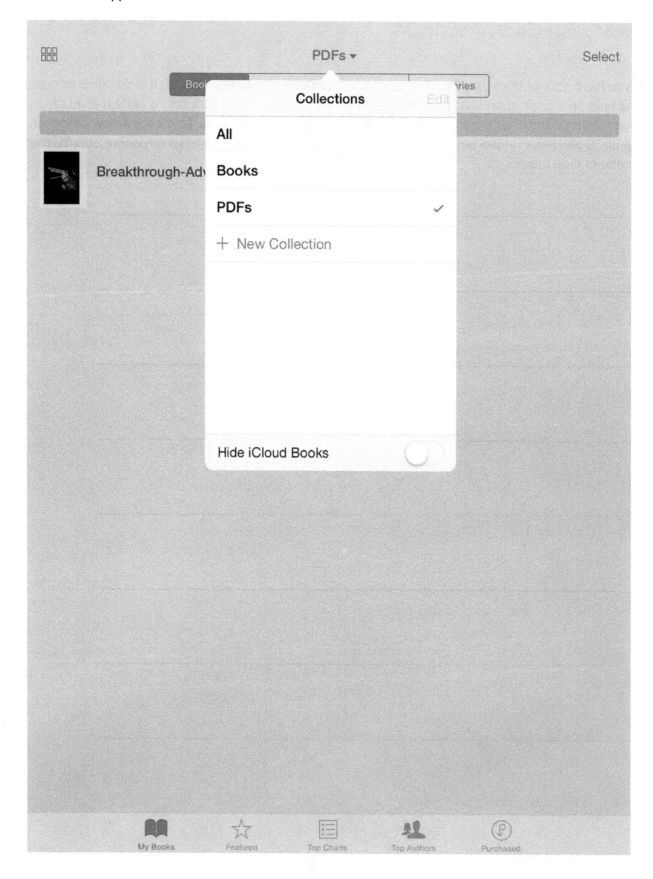

Now, press edit in the top right hand corner. Select the books you would like to move to the collection, then tap Move in the top left, and tap on the collection. You can also use the edit button to move your books around on the bookshelf. Press edit then click and drag the books to where you want them. All the books will fly into that collection. You can repeat this process until all your books are neatly organised.

To move between collections, you can either tap "Collections" then select the one you want to view, or swipe between them, although this can be slightly temperamental. Another way to view your books is by list view. Tap on the icon in the top left of the screen, and your books will rearrange themselves.

At the bottom of the screen, you will see options to sort the books by Bookshelf, Title, Author, or Category, giving you an easy way to find specific books.

Kindle app

An alternative to iBooks is the Kindle app. This allows you to buy books from Amazon, and sync your notes, bookmarks, and place in the book with your Kindle, if you have one. Firstly, you'll need to download the Kindle app from the App Store by searching for it, then pressing the button that says "Free" or "Install".

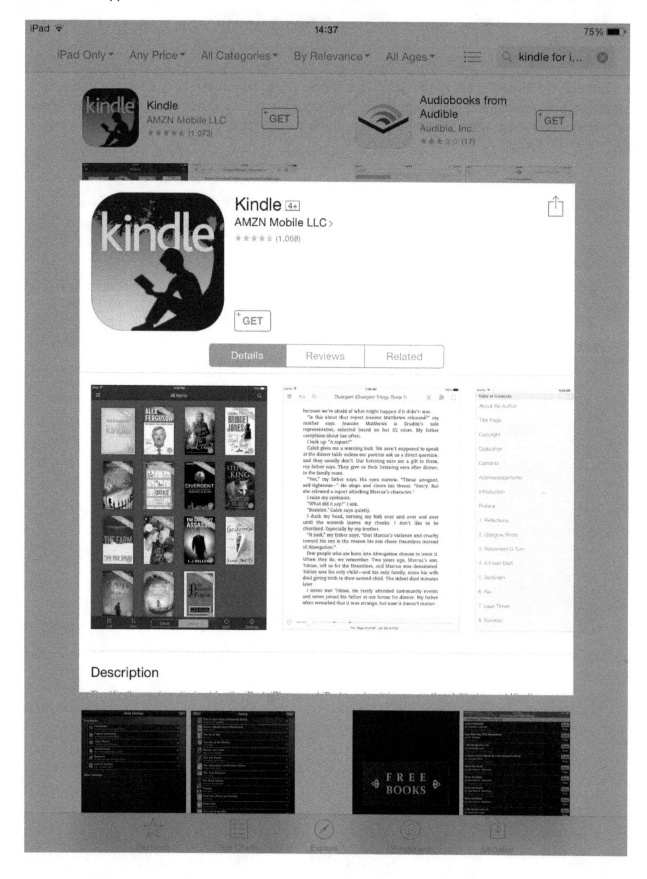

Open it when it has been downloaded, and sign in with your Amazon account. If you do not have an Amazon account, you will have to go to the Amazon website and create one.

Once you are signed in, your iPad will register with Amazon, and any books you have previously purchased through Kindle will appear. To buy more books, you need to log onto the Amazon website, either on your iPad or a laptop, find a book you would like to download, select a device to send it to, then purchase it. As with iBooks you're able to read a sample first, customise your screen layout and subscribe to various publications.

Press the refresh button in the bottom right of the Kindle app to search for available books. If you have purchased a book but haven't downloaded it to this iPad, you can do so by tapping on the arrow. Once it has downloaded, tap on the book to open it. Kindle doesn't provide a page turning animation, instead you just swipe, or tap on either side of the book, to move to the next page.

As with iBooks, you can adjust screen brightness, change text size, alter the font, and choose a theme. In addition to this, you can set how wide the text body should be. You can also search the book, scan through it using the bar at the bottom of the page, and skip to a certain chapter. Adding bookmarks and notes is very similar to iBooks. Press and hold at the start of where you want to highlight, then drag to the point you would like it to stop. Tap on the highlight to add a note, or to share it. Unfortunately, you cannot change the colour of highlights.

To bookmark a page, simply tap on the bookmark icon in the top right. You can view your notes and highlights by tapping on this icon, then selecting "My Notes and Marks". You can also open "Book Extras", which gives you notes on characters, settings, memorable quotes, and more.

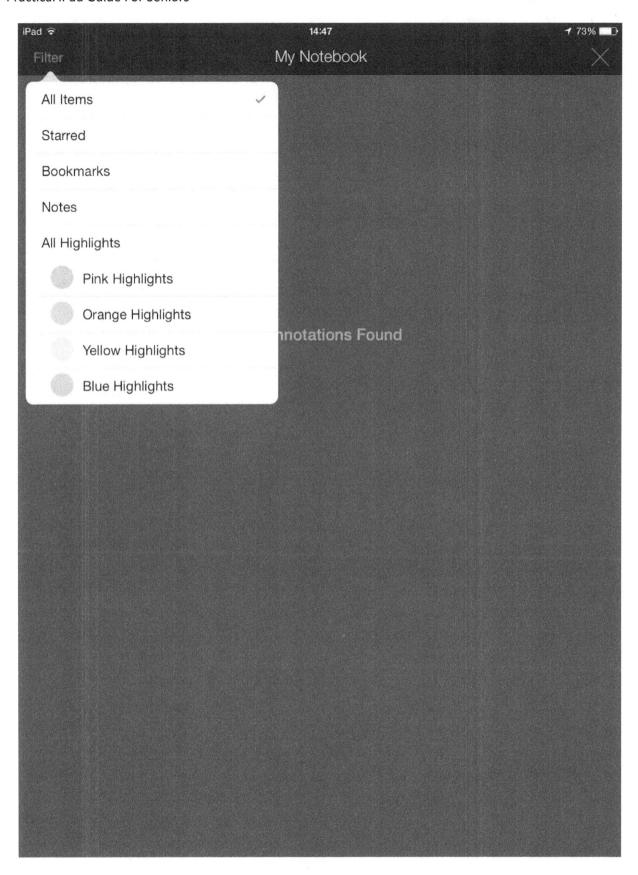

To sync your current place,bookmarks, notes, and highlights, tap on the sync button in the top right. An activity indicator will appear to show that all of your content is up to date. One final thing the Kindle app does is allow you to add your books to a number of different categories, rather than just one.

Newsstand

Newsstand is a virtual newsagent which allows you to download and read digital versions of your favorite magazines and newspapers on your iPad. You can buy subscriptions and have the latest edition of your subscription delivered to your iPad automatically. All of your subscriptions will be housed together in your Newsstand app, as it acts like a giant folder. To finds newspapers and magazines to subscribe to, open Newsstand and tap on "Store".

You will be taken to a certain section of the App Store. Here, you can browse through featured magazines, or find them through categories. If you know what you're looking for, it is possible to use the search function for magazines. Tap on "Featured" then enter your search query in the top right.

If you don't know what you're looking for, you can search the store be genre. By default, you will be searching the whole App Store, not just Newsstand. However, if you tap on "All Categories", then select "Newsstand", only Magazines and Newspapers will appear in the results.

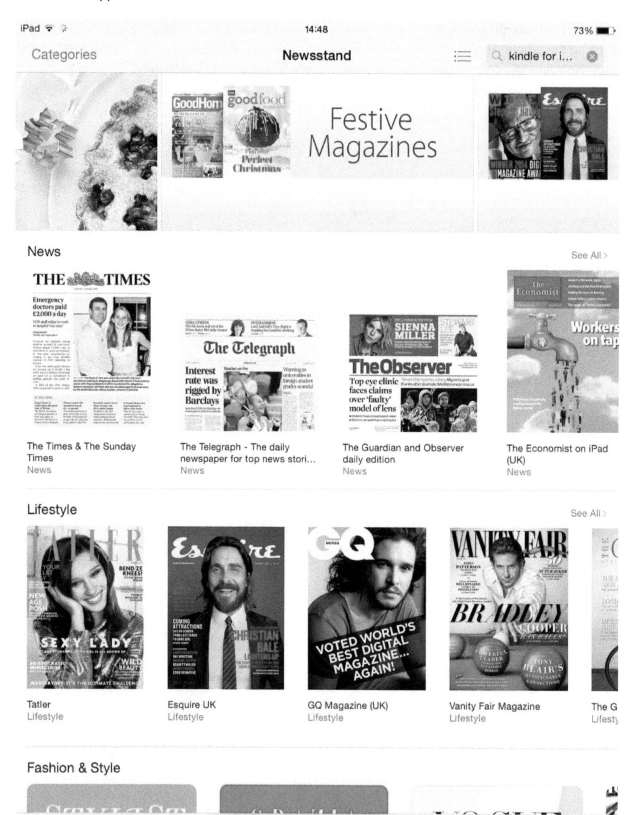

Tap on the cover of the magazine you are interested in downloading to see screenshots, a description, and ratings and reviews.

To download the magazine, tap the button which will say "Free", or display a price if you have never downloaded the magazine before, or "Install" if you have. Your magazine will begin downloading, when it has finished, tap on it to open it.

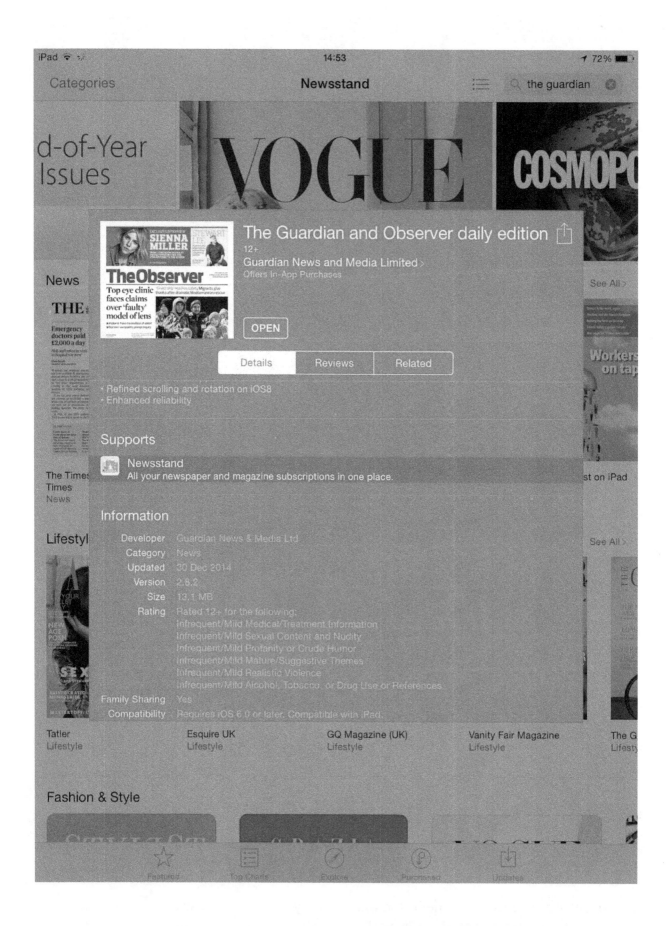

Most magazines will ask you if you want to receive push notifications. These notifications will normally let you know of special offers, or when the next issue is available.

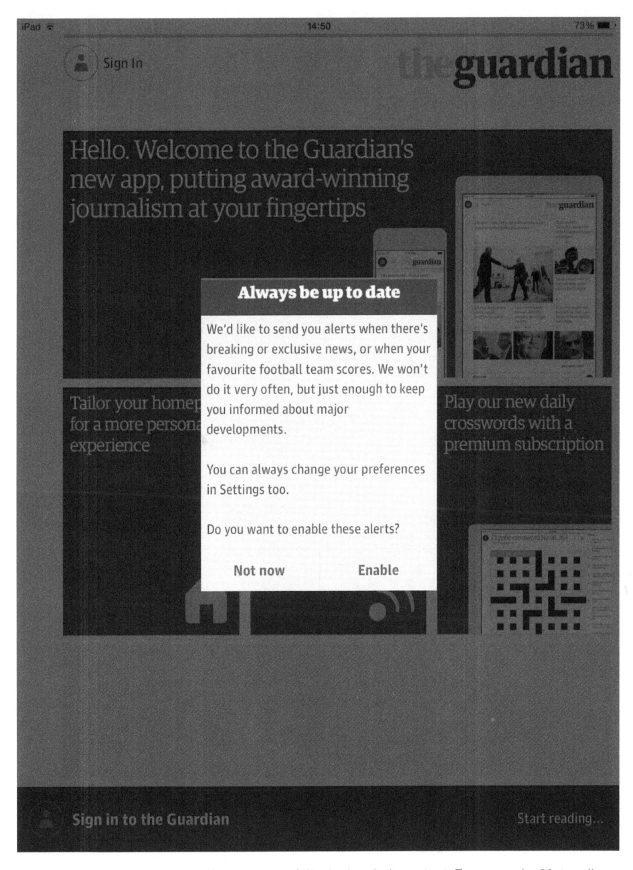

Different magazines will have different ways of displaying their content. For example, Metro allows you to download magazines individually, for free.

If you want your magazine to be downloaded automatically when a new issue is available, you will need to subscribe to it. Again, different magazines will have different ways of doing this. For free newspapers - such as Metro - it will often just be the option to subscribe, meaning magazines will be automatically downloaded until you delete the app.

For paid ones - such as the Guardian you may be offered free subscriptions for a number of editions, before you must start paying for it.

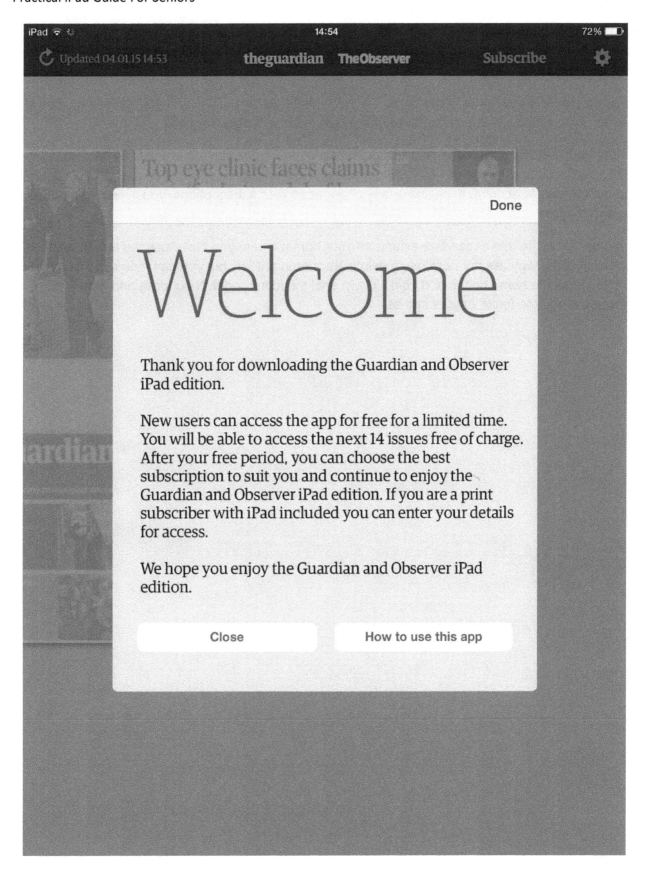

All subscriptions are managed via the app store, rather than the Newsstand app. You can get to the store via Newsstand or via the App store. You'll need to know your Apple ID in order to make a purchase. When you have opted to subscribe, you will be told how much you are paying, and be asked to confirm it. Subscriptions will automatically renew themselves until you opt to cancel them.

When you have tapped Confirm, and entered your password, you will be sent an email detailing your subscription. Make sure you read this clearly. The email will also tell you how to unsubscribe from the magazine.

Now, whenever a new issue is available, it will download automatically, and you will see an icon in the top of the magazine letting you know there is something for you to read.

To see your existing subscriptions, press on subscriptions in the app store and then "manage". Here you will be able to see all your active and expired subscriptions. Press on any subscriptions to find out the details about it. If you make any changes to your subscriptions, you'll need to input your password again.

If you don't want to use or see Newsstand on your homescreen, you can place the app in another folder out of the way. It's not possible to delete Newstand entirely but you can hide it in this way.To do this, press the home button and hold it down until the icons jiggle. Next, drag and drop Newsstand into the folder of your choice.

Watching Videos on your iPad

Buying and renting movies /TV shows

The iPad allows you to download and watch movies without having to go near a computer. Simply open the iTunes app, then tap on Films, or TV Programmes. You will be taken to a featured page, showing all the latest and best films and TV programmes. You can also use the toolbar at the top to see the different film and programme categories.

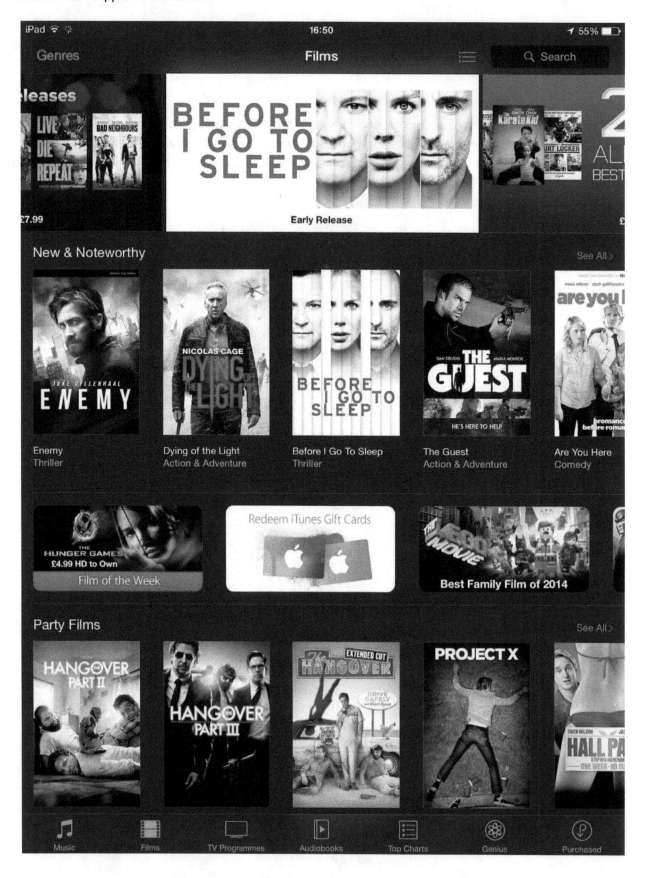

If you would like to look for something specific, search using the box in the top right. Your iPad will first search everything in the iTunes store, but when you're on this page, you can only use the bar at the top to look for films or TV programs.

When you have found the film or program you would like to download, tap on it. If it is a TV program, you will be able to download either the whole previous season, or individual episodes.

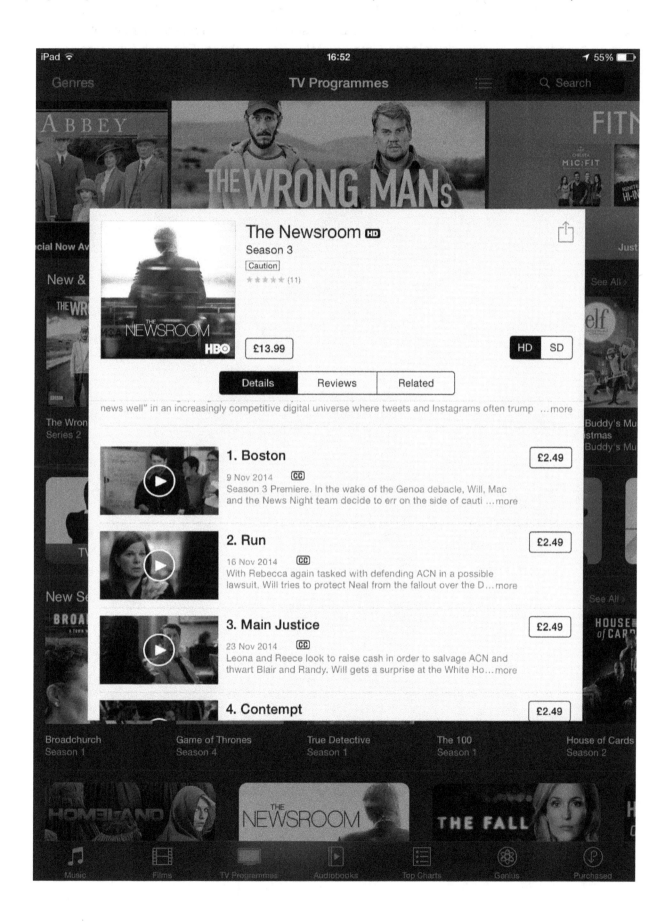

It is possible to buy a season pass for TV shows. This means you can buy the entire season of a show before all the episodes have been officially released. By ordering in this way you don't have to worry about missing an episode and quite often you'll get offered a discount to buy in this way. The season pass is only available for shows that are being shown on TV. All episodes that have been shown on broadcast TV will be downloaded immediately after purchase. For each future episode, you will be sent a notification to indicate when the latest episode has been delivered to your account.

By default, your TV show or film will download in HD, but if you are not worried about quality, you can choose to download only SD episodes. The next step of downloading it is to tap on the price, then tap Buy. The episode or series will begin downloading.

If you are instead downloading a film, you might be given the option to either buy it or rent it.

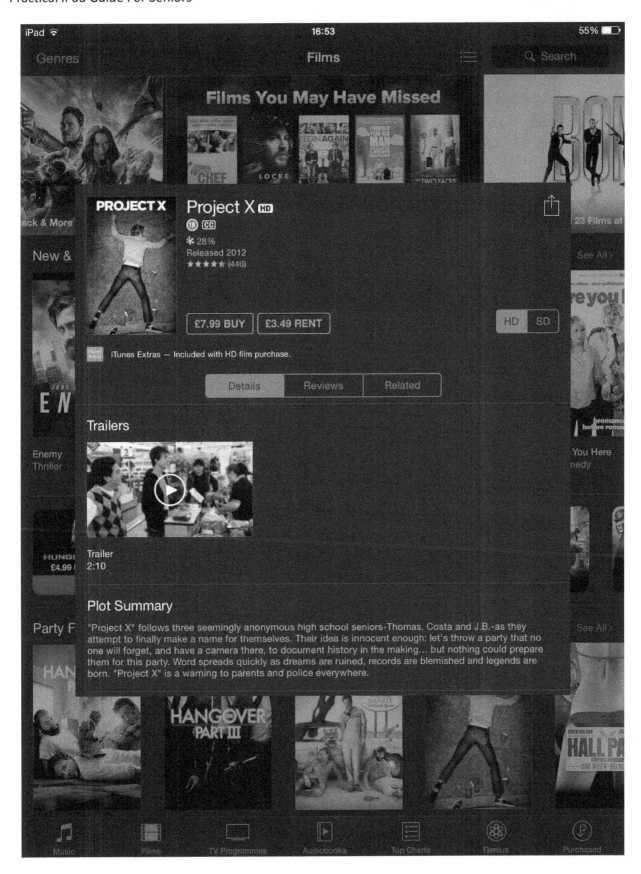

Renting means you can download a film for a much cheaper price, but keep it for a limited time. When you download it, you then have 30 days in which to watch the film for the first time. Following the first time you press play, you can watch the film as many times as you like within the next 24 hours in the US, or 48 hours elsewhere in the world. If you'd like to then share the TV show, press the share button in the top right hand corner of the iTunes store app. This will publicise the show details to whomever you want to show it to. You can either copy the link or share via a number of social media outlets such as Facebook or Twitter

After this time period has ended, the film will be removed from your device, and to watch it again you will either have to buy it, or rent it a second time.As with TV programmes, you can download or rent the film in High Definition or Standard Definition, with the latter giving you a reduced price.

Transferring videos to/from computer

If you have purchased films on your computer, or have home videos you would like to transfer to your iPad, you can do so via iTunes. To transfer home videos, open iTunes, then navigate to Films. From here you can press file, Add to Library, then select the video you would like to add. This will then be copied into your iTunes library.

Once it has imported, open your iPad's settings, then navigate to films in the top toolbar. Tick the Sync Films checkbox, and then tick the films you would like to be transferred to your iPad. You can also select to automatically include all films, or a few of your most recent unwatched films. When you are done, click apply. Your iPad will sync, and your transferred films will appear on your iPad in the Videos app, ready for you to play.

How to play other video formats

The iPad only supports certain formats of videos. The easiest way to watch these on your iPad is to download a free converter on your Mac or PC, convert the videos, and then transfer them via iTunes. Failing that there are a few good third party apps that will do the job. Two of them are AVPlayer HD and Cinexplayer HD. The latter will play files stored on your iPad and the former will allow a transfer of files to your iPad using WiFi or a USB cable connection from iTunes. Launch iTunes and tap on your iPad when it appears, then click on apps. Next tap on "file sharing" and choose AVplayer HD or Cinexplayer HD. Finally tap on + to add files.

Third party Apps that doesn't Cost Money

YouTube

With iOS 6, Apple removed the default YouTube app from the iPad. Now you have the choice of either using the YouTube website, or downloading Google's free YouTube app from the App Store. To download the app, simply search for YouTube in the App Store.

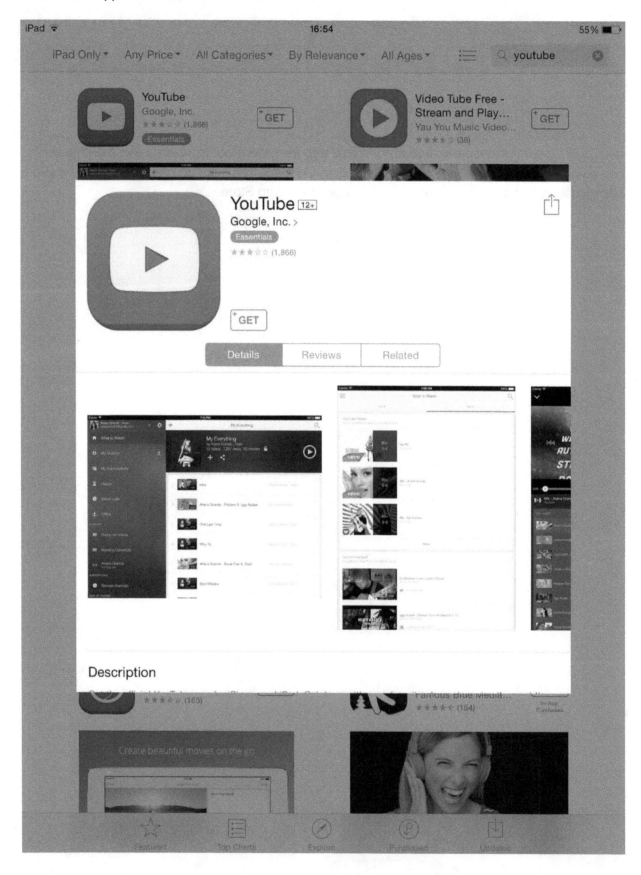

If you have a YouTube account, tap on this icon, then tap sign in and enter your details. You will then be shown your subscriptions. Tap on any video to view it. You can also make the video full screen and, if available, turn on subtitles. Below the video, you will see details of the video, with the options to like, dislike, and share the video, as well as the comments section and suggested videos. The videos can be shared via Facebook, Twitter, Google + and email

You don't have to stop watching videos to search for the next one either. If you want to search for videos, you can use the search bar to type in text, or search with your voice by pressing the microphone button.

If you want to view your playlists, such as favourites or watch later, uploads, history, and more, swipe right anywhere in the app. A sidebar will appear,

showing all your subscriptions. Tap on your name to open a menu, then select the playlist you would like to view. All videos in it will then appear on the screen, ready for you to play. To sign out from the app, open the sidebar again, tap on settings, then tap sign out.

Finally, if you're looking for a great editing app, that will help you get your film ready to upload to youtube. iMovie makes the editing process very simple.

Streaming videos from PC

Sometimes you may not want to transfer videos to your iPad in order to save space. If this is the case, you can still watch them on your iPad by streaming them from your computer. One of the best ways of doing this is through VLC.

VLC is a free app for both PC and Mac, which you can download from the internet. When you have downloaded the VLC player, open the App Store on your iPad, and search for VLC.

One of the top results will be VLC Streamer. There is a free and a paid version. When you open the app, it will tell you that you need a helper installed on your computer. Tap 'Yes, Send me details', enter your email address, and follow the instructions in the email to download and install the helper.

Your iPad and your computer must be on the same wireless network in order for it to work. On your iPad, your computer should then appear. Tap on it, then tap 'add a movie'. You can then navigate your computer's directory, and select the video you want to watch. When you have tapped on it, dismiss the browser window, and select the quality you would like to view the video in. If you know you have a fast network, select high or very high resolution, but otherwise normal resolution should be fine. When you have selected the resolution, tap 'Watch!'. A loading window will appear, and then your video will start playing.

Flash on the iPad

One of the biggest gripes with the iPad is its lack of Flash. This means that certain websites will not be visible on the iPad, and certain YouTube videos will not be playable. To get around this, you can download the free Puffin Browser from the App Store.

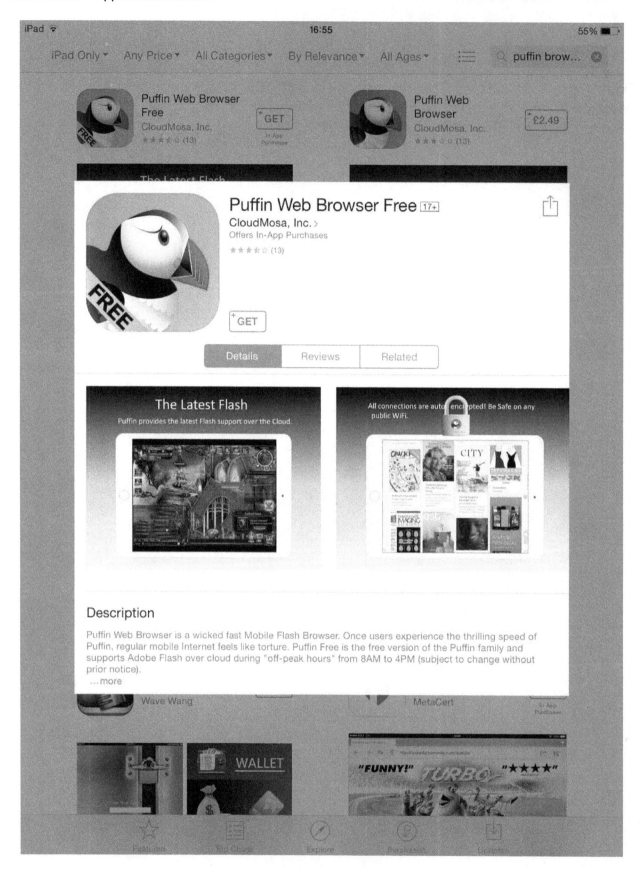

The flash support is also free for only for two weeks, after that you'll need to pay for it. Simply search for Puffin Browser, and download it. When it has downloaded, open the app. You can then navigate to any website you wish, just as you would in Safari. Sites that use Flash, such as YouTube, will now be viewable on your iPad.

There are a couple of issues with the Puffin browser. Although it's among the fastest, it's still a bit slow. Also not all Flash applications are viewable on the iPad, and not all of them work well with a touch screen. However, using the Puffin Browser is definitely better than having no Flash at all.

TV guide app

There are many different TV guide apps available for the iPad. One of the best is ON AIR. Search for ON AIR in the App Store, then download the app. When you open the app, you will be given the option to start an assistant that will help you customize the app to suit you. Follow all the steps to suit you, until you get to the Facebook Connect section. If you would like to use this, it makes it easy to share your favorite shows to Facebook. It also means you can sync your settings between multiple devices. You will then be shown a screen with highlights relevant to the settings you have made.

There are also other screens that help you see what you want. ON AIR allows you to see what is currently playing on TV. Overview gives you a grid view of all your favorite channels, and search allows you to search the TV schedule for certain programs.

If you tap on a programme in any of the screens, you will be given detailed information about it, as well as the option to find relevant YouTube videos, tweets about the program, and show times for all other episodes. You can also share the program, rate it, and set reminders that will alert you when it is about to begin.

Netflix

If you want a huge selection of TV shows and films, past and present, via your iPad, a cost-effective way of doing so is by downloading the Netflix app. Netflix will provide with a large choice of programmes and movies. You can browse by genre and the playback is excellent quality. Once you start rating the films you watch on it, the app will build up a user profile and be able to offer you a selection of things to watch that it believes you will like, based on your ratings.

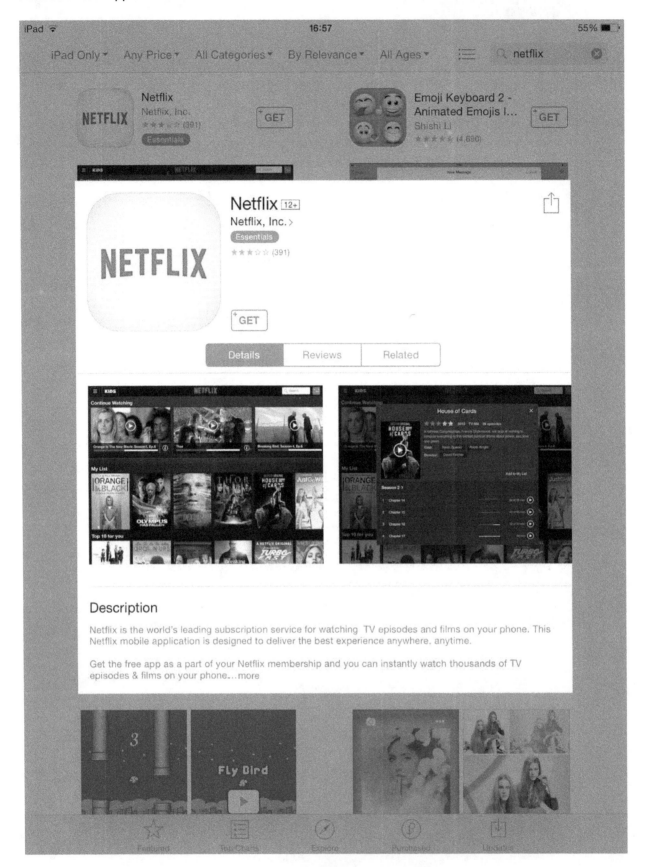

Video Podcasts

You'll need to download the "podcast app for ios" and connect to WiFi in order to stream the podcast and watch it. By streaming it via WiFi, you won't need to store it on your iPad. Go into the app and tap on "browse". Find the podcast you want to watch and tap on it to play it.

If you'd rather watch it without connecting to WiFi, you'll need to download the podcast first. Instead of tapping "play", tap "download" instead. If you tap "subscribe" the podcasts will be downloaded automatically for you. The latest episode will download when you are connected to the internet and will appear here, in "my podcasts".

iTunes U

iTunes U is a great resource for free courses in just about any subject you could imagine. Many universities, such as Stanford, upload their lectures to iTunes U, as well as setting homework and various tasks for you to do. This means you can partake in a course in your own time, and fit it around your job and personal life. To begin, you will need to download the iTunes U app by searching 'iTunes U' in the App Store.

When it has downloaded, open it, and you will be given

the option to sync your iTunes U content with your Apple ID. This means that you can use iTunes U on your iPad, iPhone, iPod, and Mac, and all your content will remain in sync. You can tap on the 'Catalogue' button to view courses available.

You will be shown an interface very similar to the iTunes and App Stores. The main screen is a featured section for all categories, but you can filter this by using the top toolbar. You will also see the option to view the Top Charts, displaying the current most popular courses and collections.

You can also search for courses. When you find one that interests you, tap on it. You can then subscribe to it, as well as downloading individual bits of course content.

When you have subscribed, it will appear in your library. Tap on it to open, and you will be given a notebook style view of the course. Use the 'Info' button in the top toolbar to view different bits of information about the course. If you tap on 'Posts', you can see an entire outline of the course, which you can follow along with.

Tap on videos to stream them, or press the download button to download them onto your device for later viewing. When you are viewing videos, you can tap on this button in the toolbar to take notes while you watch. These notes will show up in the notes section. When you are finished with a video, tick the box to show you have viewed it. You can also view course material – again, either by tapping on it or downloading on it – and read through assignments.

Tick everything as you go means that you will be able to keep track of your progress. The materials section allows you to view all of the course materials available to download and watch. You also have the option to filter materials by their type, and to turn on Auto Download, which means all new content will automatically appear on your iPad. To exit a course, tap the Library button at any time.

Navigating With Maps

Map application and GPS

The iPad comes with a free Maps application that offers map data across the globe.

Open the Maps application, then tap on the screen to view your

current location. You will be shown the view from overhead. The app may ask for permission to do so, if you haven't connected location services.

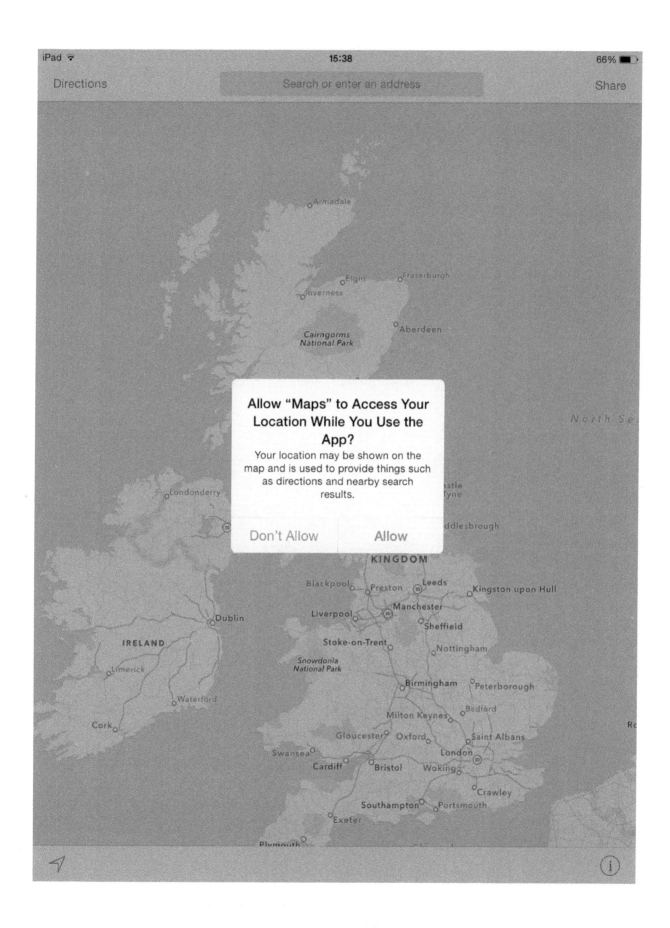

iPads with WiFi and 3G have a GPS chip, which allows them to give incredibly accurate location data. WiFi-only iPads will use WiFi to try and get an accurate estimate of your current location.

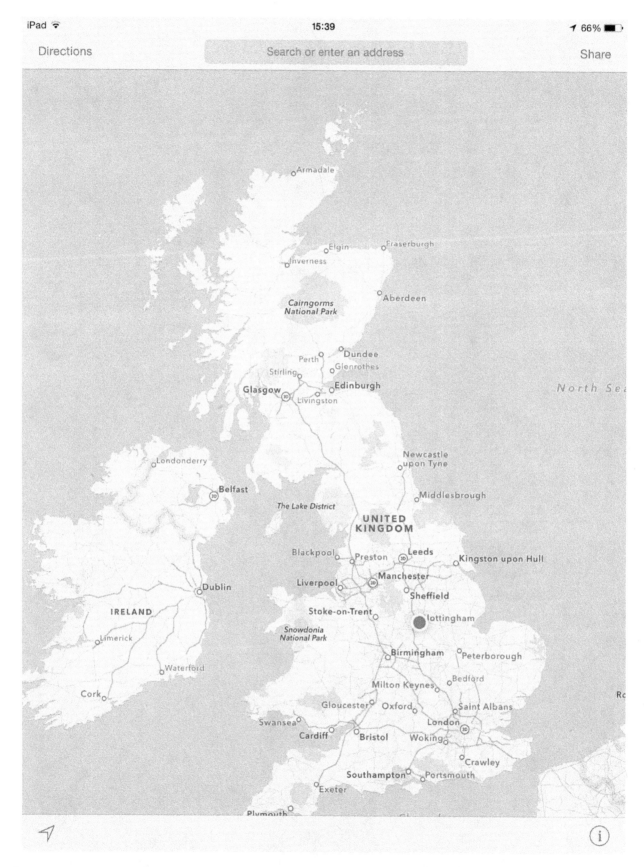

As you can see, on your map screen you will be give a number of options. You can plan a route, search for locations, bookmark, centre yourself, turn on 3D maps and share your location via iMessages, Twitter or Facebook. You can select any of these by tapping on them.

Gestures on maps

There are some gestures you can use in maps. Pinch to zoom in and out of the map. You can also use two fingers to rotate the map. In addition to this, if you tap on the location icon again, you will be able to make the map automatically orientate to the direction you are facing.

Search

To search for places, enter the place name in the search bar. Suggestions may appear, and when you have entered the place you want, press return and you should be taken there.

The default map view looks like this.

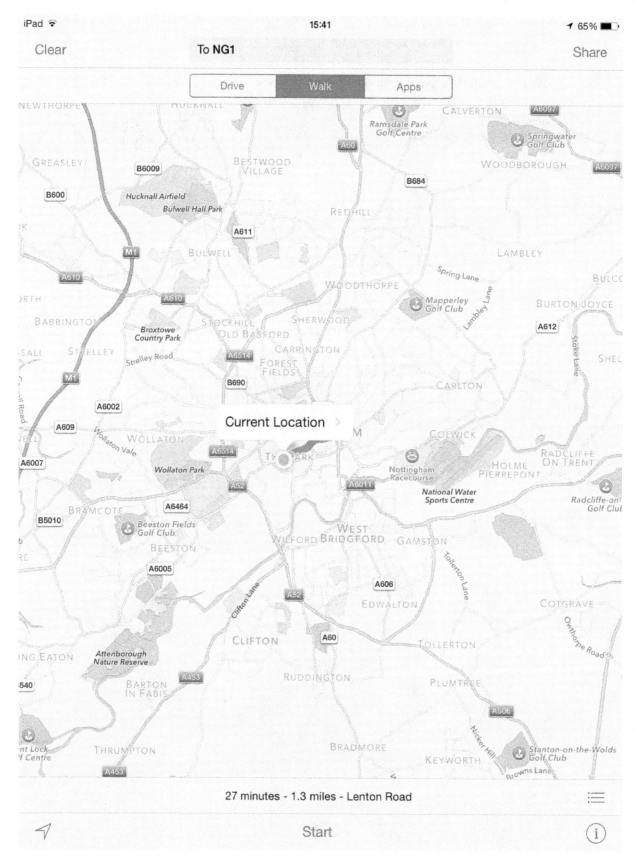

By pressing the info button, you can change it to Hybrid – which shows road data overlayed on satellite imagery –

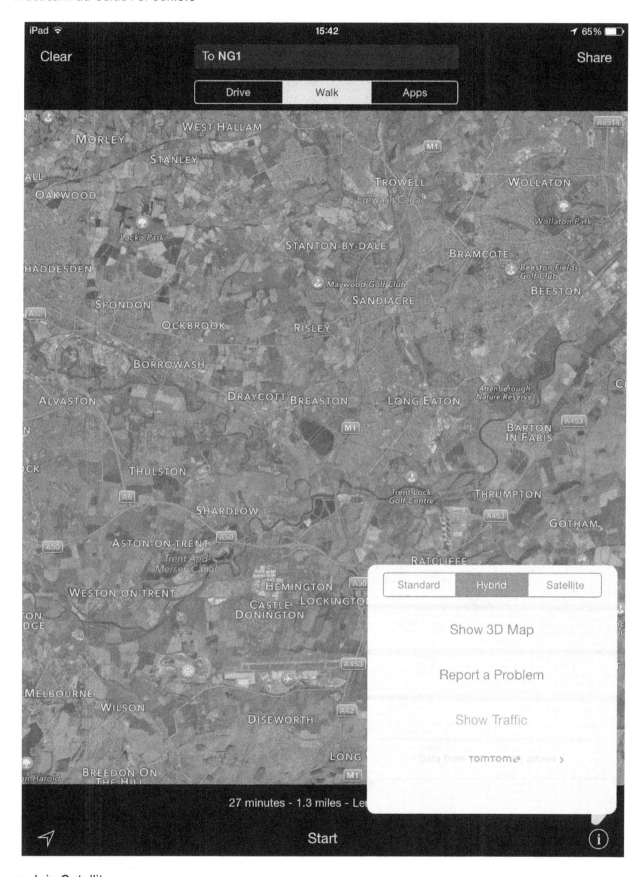

or plain Satellite.

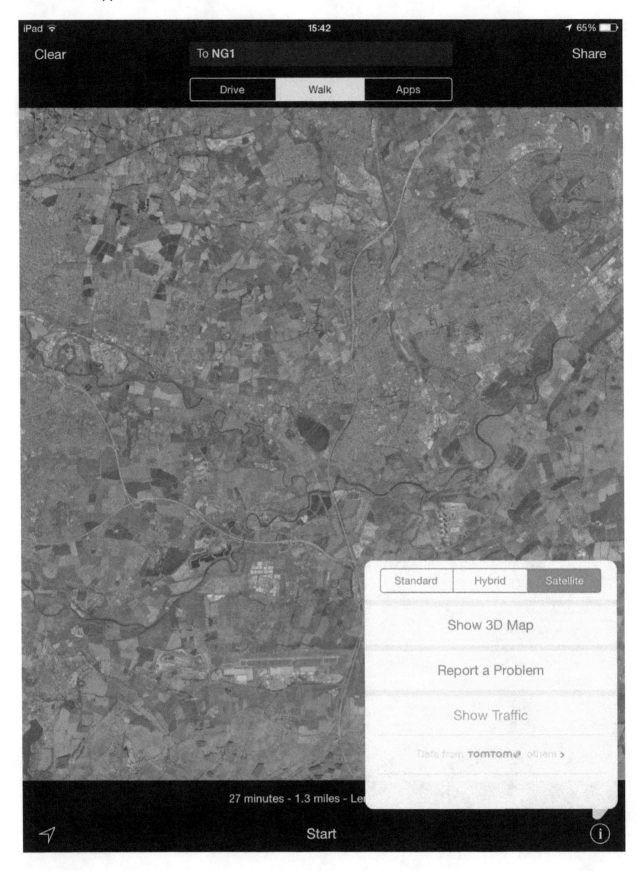

The quality of this imagery will vary depending on your area. Also on this menu, you will find the option to drop a pin, get traffic information, print the map out and report a problem. Tap on any option to select. To leave this menu, tap on the map. This will reveal a full screen view of the map.

Traffic View & Street View

Traffic view will allow you to see the current state of traffic conditions. Information about the traffic in a given area will be overlaid on a map. Tap on the button that says "Show traffic." Any roads with slow-moving traffic will now be displayed with a dashed red line.

Street View

Street view is a type of 3D mapping. You can look at the street ahead, behind you and side to side as if you were standing on it. Street view is not available for everywhere, a blue line will indicate where it is available. You can also drag a "**pegman**" icon onto the map. A solid line will show you which way street view continues in order for you to view further. To turn on 3D mapping or street view, you'll need to turn on either satellite or hybrid, then navigate to one of these locations.

If you drag upwards with two fingers. You will now see that all of the buildings are in 3D. You can zoom in to see more detail, and even use two fingers to spin around buildings.

Route Planning

Now let's have a look at route planning, when you know where you want to go. Type your start and end addresses into the search bar. Maps will automatically provide you with driving directions but this will change if you select walking or public transport. More about this in a minute. You may be given a choice of routes. Tap any route to view its details.

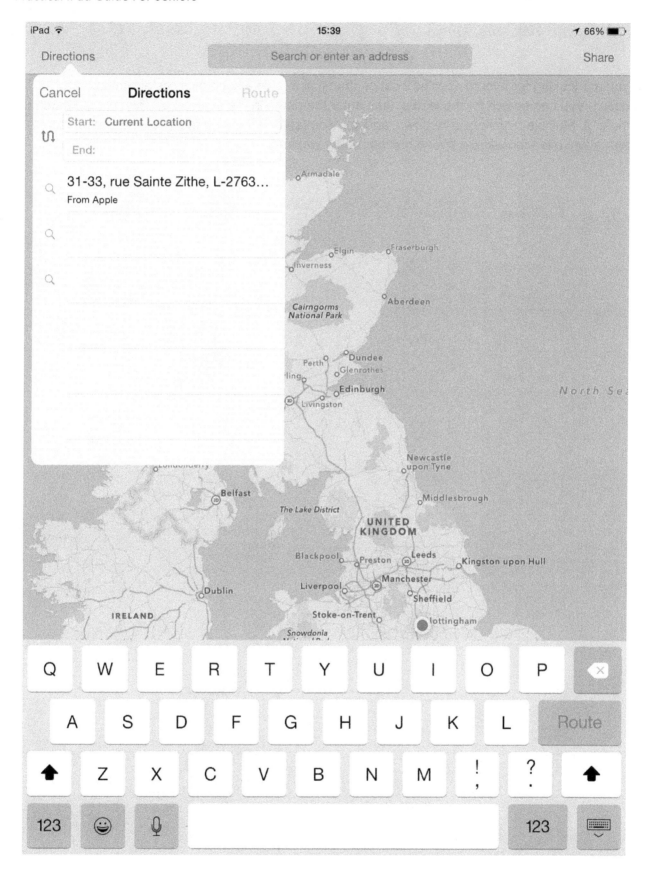

Finding and bookmarking

If you are looking for a more specific location than just a town – such as a restaurant and train station – you can search for these, too. Just enter the name in the search bar, then press search to look for it. Multiple pins may drop down, and you can tap one, then on the 'i' icon to see more information, often including a phone number and a website.

You can tap the 'add to bookmarks' button to make it easier to find in future. If you see suggested locations popping up automatically in your search bar while you are searching, these will be based on recent searches or addresses pulled from your iMessages

If there is something you would like to save that is not listed, zoom in on the location, then press and hold. A pin will drop, and you can add it as a bookmark in the same way. Now, simply tap on the bookmarks button, and you will be able to navigate to any of your saved places.

Search and Navigation

Once you have found the place you would like to go to, you need to get directions. Tap on any pin – either one you have found through searching, one of your bookmarks, or one you have dropped yourself then tap on the green car icon. This will immediately give you driving directions to your location, often with a choice of multiple routes. Tap on each route to see how long it will take, and how far it is.

When you have picked one, press start. You will then see large directions appear at the top of the screen. Swipe on these to move backwards and forwards between directions.

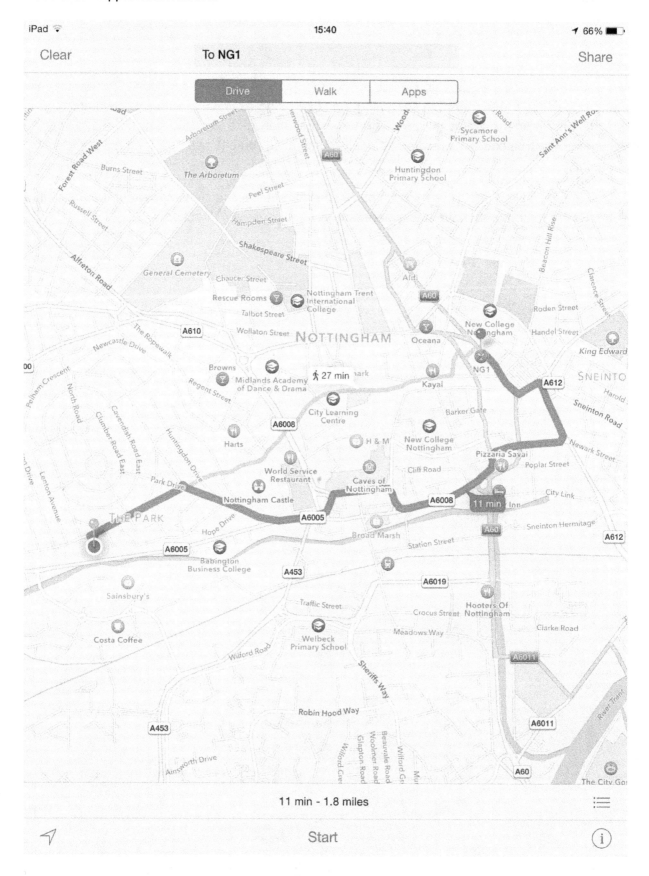

If you tap the 'Overview' button to see your entire route, then tap on the button in the bottom left to see a list of all your directions. You can also change from a list of directions back into map view by pressing the buttons with the three lines at the bottom.

If you would like to get walking directions instead of driving ones, you will have to get them in a different manner. Press end to exit the current set of directions. Then, tap on the Directions button, enter your start and end destinations, then tap on the walking icon in the top toolbar. Press 'Route' and you will be given directions.

These work in exactly the same way as the driving directions, only the time estimate will be relevant to walking rather than driving.

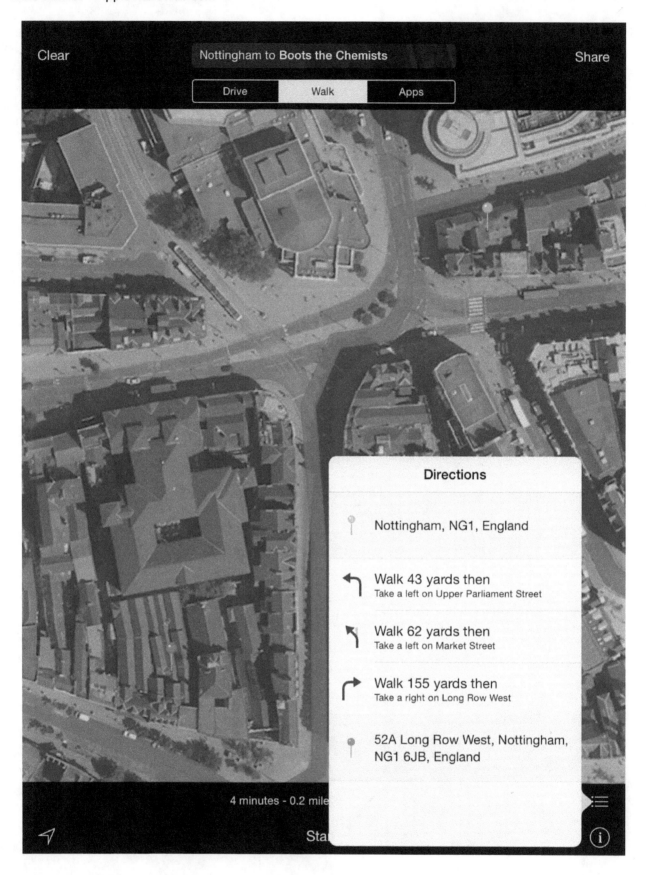

A final option is transport directions. When you press route, you will be given a list of apps that can offer you public transport directions between those locations. Download one of these – many are free – and wait for it to install. When it has installed, you can ask for directions again, and a Route button will appear. Tap on it to be taken to that app.

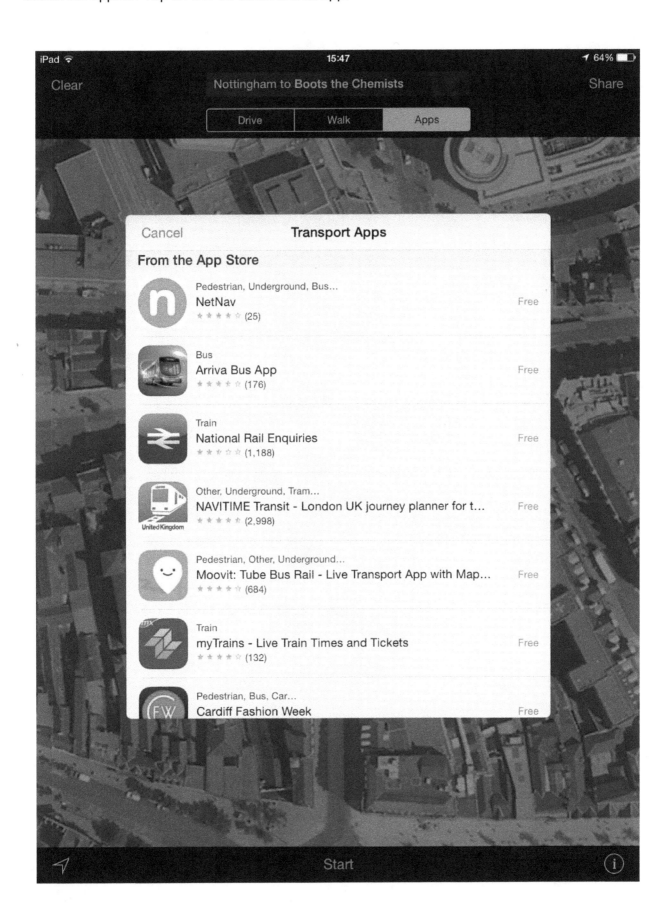

Finally it's worth knowing that at night the screen colours will change automatically into night mode, with the map appearing in darker colours allowing for you to see it better in the dark.

Thank You For Reading !

Dear Reader

I hope you enjoyed "Practical iPad Guide For Seniors". I really like working with my iPad and hope this guide will serve as a reference guide and help you get the most out of your iPad. Though many readers wrote to me asking, "What's Next". Well stay tuned because another guide book covering most popular apps will soon be released.

I got many letters from readers thanking me for the book. Some went through the book in few hours and learnt all at once while others use it as a reference guide and learn as they go along. As an author I love feedback. Honestly you are the reason that I will release future guide books. So tell me what you liked, what you loved, what you hated, I'd love to hear from you. You can write to me at support@applevideohub.com and visit me on the web at www.applevideohub.com

Finally I need to ask you a favor. If you're so inclined, I'd love a review of "Practical iPad Guide For Seniors" Liked it or Hated it, I'd just enjoy your feedback.

Reviews are really hard to come by these days. You the reader, have the power now to make or break a book. If you have time, you can check all my guide books at my author page.

Thank you so much for reading this book.

In gratitude

Mike Jeffries

www.ingramcontent.com/pod-product-compliance
Lightning Source LLC
Chambersburg PA
CBHW080152060326
40689CB00018B/3950